Preface

MANY introductory textbooks of parasitology assume the classical taxonomic approach, dealing with the different zoological groups of parasites in turn. Such books provide good works of reference but demand that the reader conquer a great number of facts and may make the whole study of parasites seem somewhat obscure, distant, and theoretical. In fact it is quite the contrary. The principal intention of this book is to suggest some of the fascination of the topic and to point out its central relevance to the study of zoology.

It discusses in general terms, and with the minimum amount of technicality, what parasites are, how they live, and the factors important to their ecology. Theoretical aspects of parasitism, including host specificity, transmission, evolution, and geographical distribution are discussed, and where possible these topics are compared with general biological phenomena and with free-living organisms.

I should like to express my thanks to Professor B. G. Peters for his critical reading of the manuscript and for the many useful suggestions he offered. I am also indebted to my wife and colleagues for the stimulus of discussion they so often granted me, in particular Messrs J. J. M. Flegg and T. S. C. Orr, and Dr R. A. Wilson. Thanks are also due to Mrs Z. M. Croll for kindly typing the draft manuscript and to Messrs W. H. Dowdeswell and Hamish MacGibbon for their willing co-operation in the business of publication.

For permission to reproduce photographs, I wish to thank Dr H. H. Williams (Plate 2), Dr F. Hawking (Plate 4(b)), Dr Chubb (plate 3(b)), Dr R. Muller (Plate 4(a)), and Mr R. A. Ashford for kindly supplying the specimens in Plate 1(b).

PREFACE

Finally I must, of course, accept all responsibility for the arguments and opinions in the text. I do however beg the indulgence of the hypercritical, as valid generalizations in biology are rare, and for the sake of clarity I have perhaps drawn some unqualified conclusions and disregarded the rare exceptions.

THE SCHOLARSHIP SERIES IN BIOLOGY

General Editor: W. H. Dowdeswell

ECOLOGY OF PARASITES

ECOLOGY
OF
PARASITES

by

N. A. CROLL, B.Sc., Ph.D., A.R.C.S.

Director of the Institute of Parasitology
McGill University

HEINEMANN EDUCATIONAL BOOKS

LONDON

Heinemann Educational Books Ltd
LONDON EDINBURGH MELBOURNE AUCKLAND TORONTO
SINGAPORE HONG KONG KUALA LUMPUR
IBADAN NAIROBI JOHANNESBURG
LUSAKA NEW DELHI

ISBN 0 435 61190 9

Published by
Heinemann Educational Books Ltd
48 Charles Street, London W1X 8AH
Printed Offset Litho and bound in Great Britain by
Cox & Wyman Ltd, London, Fakenham and Reading

Contents

List of Plates

1

The Problem of Definition

IT is characteristic of man, and certainly of biologists, to classify and define, and many reasons can be given for doing so, but there are also important dangers. Taxonomic systems and other biological groupings created by scientists are attempts to produce workable schemes which correspond to existing natural systems. The policy of producing these schemes correctly, is most desirable. It is, however, equally undesirable to *impose* a distinction where no distinction exists in nature. The creation of artificial boundaries and categories is a frequent failing of workers concerned with animal associations as often these correspond to no distinct natural groupings.

The division between plants and animals tends to disappear when certain of the protozoa are studied; similarly, the age-old boundary separating living and non-living becomes more speculative in the light of our knowledge of viruses. How much more arbitrary must be the definitions of animal associations, associations between two variable and distantly-related creatures, which may have any relationship within an almost *unlimited range* of intimacy or dependence on one another.

At the time when the chief categories of association were being named, there was perhaps evidence to suggest that certain levels of intimacy between organisms could be grouped under separate headings. As research continued, however, and knowledge increased, the actual nature of the relationships was studied for the first time and many of the original assumptions had to be questioned and some were disproved. For example, the minute protozoa and bacteria so essential for the digestive processes of ruminants, were originally thought to be parasites.

This increase in knowledge has caused some authors to

create more and more categories of animal association with finer and finer distinctions; this is not the approach of the present writer. It is argued here that the continual discovery of intermediaries and of linking types must break down a system that is thereby shown to be artificial.

To impose artificial barriers, which apparently do not correspond to natural limits, is unscientific and misleading, but to follow tendencies, or to list general characteristics is often helpful. In this section, three general groupings are recognized (out of a possible fifteen or more established by some authors); these three are considered only in the most general way and are not intended to be exclusive or to have well-defined limits. They are 'Commensalism', 'Symbiosis' and 'Parasitism'.

Two criteria often used to distinguish between types of animal associations are: the relative loss or gain from the association, and the degree of dependence of one or both partners on the other. Unfortunately, the degree of dependence or benefit is rarely decided by experimental evidence; more usually the association is classified on circumstantial evidence alone.

Another difficulty arises from the literary meaning of the names given to the groupings. Symbiosis, now treated as a definite type of association by many authors, literally means 'living together' (sym = together, bios = life). In the literal sense, all animal associations are symbiotic and some authors have further complicated the issue by reverting to the original meaning.

Commensalism literally means 'together at the table' (co = together, mensa = table). This implies, that the bond between the organisms is based on feeding habits; although this is often the case, commensalism is not exclusive of other intimacies. Parasitism is equally as vague in its literal translation meaning 'beside food' (para = beside, sitos = food). A meaning adopted from the Ancient Greeks who described a person who came to dinner uninvited as a parasite.

It is obvious that too much weight must not be placed on derivational meanings and to revert to the original meaning in the case of symbiosis, while retaining special meanings for the others, is a little unwise. Let us accept these names as suitable symbols and attempt to list any general characteristics which tend to differentiate between them.

Following the above review of the difficulties, let us examine, with examples, the significance of the three major groupings and, where relevant, let us include intermediate linking associations underlining the futility of absolute distinctions.

The most indefinite and least obligatory association is commensalism; in this category there may be mutual benefit or the advantage may be one-sided (if so, it is likely that the non-benefiting organism loses something). Often one of the associates is always found with the other, while the second may or may not be found in association, suggesting that the association is necessary for one but not for both species. A well-documented example of a commensal relationship is that of the anemones *Adamsia palliata* and *Calliactis parasitica* on the adopted shell of the hermit crab *Eupagurus*. In these cases the anemones are found growing extensively over the shell and possibly even replacing it altogether. It is thought that the anemones benefit from the scraps of food left by the crab's feeding and the crab is protected by the tentacles and stinging cells of the anemones while at the same time, being camouflaged by them. The anemones are rarely found apart from the crab but the crab is often found on its own. This suggests that the anemones are more dependent on the crab than is the crab on the anemones. However, recent experiments with some hermit crabs and anemones have shown that if crab and anemone are put into a tank together, the crab will actively place the anemone on its shell. Perhaps the crab really benefits more, but since there is a 'shortage' of anemones they are always found in association.

A lesser-known but equally interesting example is the association between the common yellow ant, *Lasius flavus*, and the tiny white isopod crustacean, *Platyarthrus hoffmanseggi*. If the ants' nest is dug up, it is quite possible that this very small white woodlouse will be found. The isopod has free passage throughout the nest and enjoys the complete protection of the ants. In return, it feeds on the ant excreta and browses on the fungal hyphae which tend to grow in the warm environment of the anthill. The basis of this arrangement is ecological, the ant 'acknowledging' its need for a refuse-collector-cum-gardener and, in turn, tolerating the isopod's intrusion.

There are many other examples of commensalism, including tick birds and cattle egrets that sit on the backs of antelope and feed on their ectoparasites, and the pilot fish which guide sharks about and feed on any scraps that chance to come their way. Such associations tend to be ecological and do not involve dependence, and the benefit would appear to be mutual in most cases.

Symbiosis is the next general category to be considered and here it has more than just its literal meaning. Symbiosis applies to an association (between plants or animals), where both organisms are always found together, depending on each other for their existence. (It may be mentioned here that *P. hoffmanseggi* and the anemones on the hermit crab – although commensals – are always found in partnership.) The following examples of symbiotic associations include some of the few actually endorsed by experimental evidence.

Herbivores such as ruminants that chew the cud feed exclusively on plant material, and yet they are themselves unable to digest most of it. Plant cell walls are made of cellulose and hemicelluloses and the ruminant is not equipped with the necessary enzymes to break down these complex polysaccharides.

Many years ago it was found that ruminants harboured unique protozoa, chiefly ciliates, which were then considered to be parasites. But modern biochemical investigations have shown that these symbiotic protozoans do, in fact, digest the cellulose in the ruminant's diet. The ciliates can only survive in an anaerobic environment; such an environment is to be found in the rumen and reticulum (two of the four parts of the stomach) of the ruminant, and that is where the symbionts live. The protozoa themselves feed on the cellulose and break it down into simpler compounds which the 'host' can degrade further or assimilate directly. The relationship in this case between mammal and protozoan, is one of mutual dependence at a very intimate level of biochemistry (see Fig. 1).

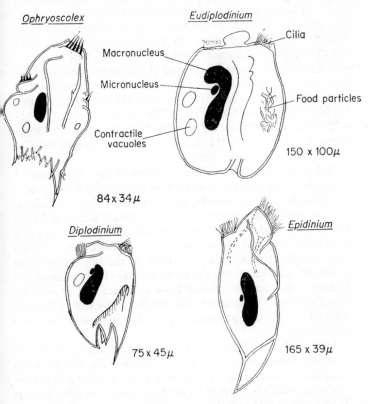

FIG. 1. Rumen Ciliates. Originally considered as parasites, more recent work has shown that some of them are important in cellulose digestion. They are strict anaerobes and are found in the rumen of ungulates. If collected from a slaughter house in a Thermos flask they can be studied alive.

Of added interest to the student of animal associations are the inter-relationships of the protozoan fauna of different ruminants. It is found that the relationships between the mammals is almost exactly replicated in the relationships of their specific protozoans. Data of this kind are useful in speculations concerning the interrelations of ruminants such as the cow, sheep, deer, elk, and moose. The phenomenon of particular organisms occurring in hosts peculiar to themselves is termed host specificity, and is dealt with later in a separate chapter.

The rabbit, also a herbivore and also unable to digest cellulose, has a considerable bacterial fauna in the caecum of its hind gut. These bacteria break down cellulose but, as this happens in the posterior region of the gut, much of the advantage is lost, the partially digested food passing out in the droppings. This is probably the chief reason for the rabbit's habit of refection (eating its own faeces).

Still concerned with cellulose digestion but far removed from mammals, are the wood-eating insects, the termites and woodroaches. These insects, also unable to digest cellulose, harbour symbiotic protozoa for the purpose; this time flagellates of the order Hypermastigina which are up to a tenth of a millimetre long and are just visible to the unaided eye. Cleveland has spent many years working on the biology of these symbionts and has shown the intimate level of biochemical and biological association existing between insect and protozoan. Being essential to the insect, it is not surprising to find that the adaptation of the protozoan goes far beyond mere food relationship.

One of the chief genera of symbiotic flagellates is *Trichonympha*, found in the intestine of the termite *Zootermopsis augusticollis*. Cleveland has shown that the moulting hormone, 'ecdysin', which is secreted by the termite for a number of days before the actual moulting process, reaches a sufficient concentration five days prior to moulting, causing the trophozoite, or feeding stage, of *Trichonympha* to encyst (Fig. 2).

The moulting period in the insect is a time of considerable hazard to *Trichonympha*, since much of the intestinal lining of

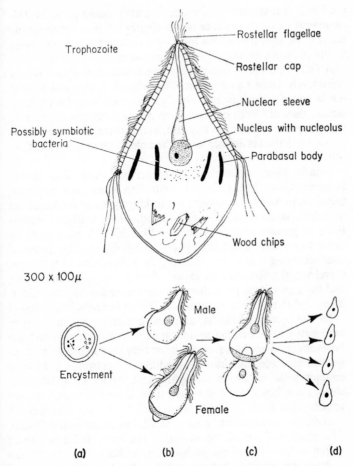

Trophozoite

Rostellar flagellae

Rostellar cap

Nuclear sleeve

Nucleus with nucleolus

Possibly symbiotic bacteria

Parabasal body

Wood chips

300 x 100μ

Encystment

Male

Female

(a)   (b)   (c)   (d)

FIG. 2. *Trichonympha campanula* from the hind gut of the termite *Zootermopis augusticollis*. The 'trophozoite' or adult feeding stage, is frequently found with wood chips inside it, which it is able to digest and therefore make the products of degradation available to the termite. Under the influence of the host moulting hormone it encysts and enters a stage of sexual multiplication.

the insect is lost with the cuticle. The association between *Trichonympha* and the termite is sufficiently intimate for the symbiont to be stimulated into forming a resistant cyst in response to the presence of host moulting hormone.

A final example of symbiosis is the association of two plants collectively known as a lichen. The lichen is a composite plant made up of a fungus and an alga: in their association as a lichen, they are both completely dependent on one another in many aspects of their biology and, in this form, they are able to survive in habitats neither would be able to tolerate without the other.

Finally, there is the problem of defining parasitism. It has been emphasized that absolute definition is unwise when dealing with animal associations; for linking types or intermediate associations must also be considered. Most textbook definitions of parasitism run something like this: 'A parasite is an animal or plant, which lives partly or wholly at the expense of another living organism, its host.' By a definition of this type, therefore, the fox may be regarded as parasitic on the rabbit and the earthworm parasitized by the thrush; it will, no doubt, be agreed that such a definition as it stands needs elaboration!

Parasites may be plants, animals, bacteria, or viruses; they are limited to no one taxonomic group; they must also do their hosts some harm, however small, or they could equally be considered one-sided symbionts. In addition, parasites must live in contact with, either on (ectoparasites), or within (endoparasites) their hosts for some period in their life cycle; and in general they must be smaller than their hosts (this excludes the example of a ruminant being parasitic on its intestinal fauna). The essence of parasitism is usually the one-sided dependence (often nutritional) of the parasite on the host.

Two less obvious but nevertheless fundamental aspects of parasitism may also be mentioned; well-adapted parasites rarely ever kill their hosts outright* and, in fact, a close

* There are cases of parasites killing their hosts outright, notably among the leeches; it would perhaps be valid to consider such a leech as a predator rather than a parasite.

examination of parasite biology, shows that they have evolved definite adaptations to avoid hyperinfestation and consequently disease or death.

Lastly, parasites frequently spend some period of each generation living an existence independent of their host.* This is itself an adaptation which avoids hyperinfestation, as it prevents the completion of a whole generation in a single host. Many parasites include a free-living stage in their life cycles but the independent stage may be spent in another host. For example, the malarial parasite *Plasmodium*, the stages of which alternate between a mosquito and man; in this case, the stages occurring in the mosquito may be considered as independent of man. Similarly, the stage present in man is independent of the mosquito.

The biological importance of this period of isolation from the host is one of the fundamental factors of parasitism, as it creates problems of survival and transmission, as well as being the period of distribution. It is perhaps from a better understanding of features like this that parasitism will be correctly defined in the future. Few comparable biological characteristics are found in commensals or symbionts.

It has been assumed that parasitism is disadvantageous to the host; in fact, there are examples of parasites which seem to benefit the host. A plant parasitic eelworm, *Heterodera rostochiensis*, if parasitic on potatoes in small numbers, produces better growth in the host than that of an uninfected plant. In all other aspects of its life, and where it is parasitic in larger numbers, this plant parasitic nematode is a complete parasite. This example of a border-line case also illustrates the fact that parasites may do damage largely as populations and rarely as individuals.

---

* Examples do exist of parasites which can apparently complete more than one generation in a single host without leaving it, but in helminths, such examples are very rare and not above suspicion. There are, however, many parasitic protozoans that can complete more than one generation – but for continued survival of the species they must be carried to another host by a vector.

Mosquitoes and midges are blood-sucking ecto-parasites: let us consider the blood-sucking insects of the swallow. During the evening a swallow feeds on its parasites, largely depending on them for its food supply. Following this, other parasites feed on the swallow; in other words, here is a host that benefits from its parasites.

It will be stressed that the parasitic niche, as with any other niche, demands a high level of specialization and, because of this, parasites might be expected to be completely dependent on their hosts. There are to be found, nevertheless, some parasites which can apparently alternate freely between the free-living and the parasitic ways of life. These include the *facultative* parasitic nematode *Strongyloides*, this worm having parasitic generations which may be followed by wholly free-living generations. Problems of definition must take account of *Strongyloides* and parasites like it; is a free-living *Strongyloides* a parasite? Similarly, are the free-living independent stages of obligate parasites to be considered as parasites, when they are themselves not parasitic?

As well as the groups that are readily recognized as parasites, there are a few other parasitic anomalies; for example, there is the question of 'brood parasitism'. Brood parasites include the well-known cuckoo and the North American cow bird. The habits of these are too familiar to require lengthy description; the adult bird lays its eggs in the nest of another bird or foster parent; this behaviour is further characterized by the fact that each bird always lays all its eggs in nests of one particular foster species. This is neither ecto-parasitism nor endoparasitism, but the brood parasite certainly lives at the expense of its host and does not kill it.

Another interesting example of parasitism is termed 'clepto-parasitism', and occurs among skuas. Skuas chase and molest other, usually smaller birds, and force them to drop their food, which the skua then eats itself. Here is another border-line case, as it fulfils some of the features of the parasitic way of life, but not others.

Parasites may be parasitic at any stage in their life; some

parasitic insects (e.g. Ichneumons) are parasites only in their larval stages; many insects and almost all of the helminths are parasitic as adults or at all stages. It is quite usual for protozoa to be parasitic throughout their lives.

One problem of particular interest in this general survey of the features and anomalies of definition is really an aesthetic rather than a scientific consideration. Is the human embryo, or the embryo of any placental mammal, an endoparasite? In this case, we find a distinct individual living inside another animal and at the complete expense of it, giving no material benefit to its parent. Perhaps it would be valid to include in our review of parasitic characteristics, that the young never parasitize the old of their own species. Perhaps this example is tending more towards cannibalism, for as far as definition will take us, the human embryo is definitely a cannibal of sorts. Sprent considers the embryo to be a 'homoparasite'.

Some authors choose to define blood-sucking ectoparasites as 'micropredators'; this merely illustrates the great confusion about exact definitions.

Although it may be said without hesitation that parasitism is an association between two organisms, beyond this very little can be defined with complete confidence. Even the short review here has shown that adherence to arbitrary definitions may be a dangerous attitude. If the reader can grasp the concept of parasitism, and its overall place in the types of associations between organisms, and can accept the vagueness of the definition, while understanding the problems, he will be on the correct road to understanding the true nature of parasitism.

2

The Range and Characteristics of Parasitic Forms

PARASITES do not form one natural phylogenetic group; instead, they draw their members from the whole of the plant and animal kingdoms. Some groups of animals are largely or wholly parasitic, e.g. Trematoda (flukes), Insecta (e.g. fleas), Cestoda (tapeworms), and Hirudinea (leeches), while other groups have only the occasional parasitic representatives, e.g. Mollusca (snails, slugs), Coelenterata (e.g. jellyfishes and anemones), and Crustacea. Every major group of animals, apart from the Echinodermata (starfish and sea urchins) includes at least a few parasites in their ranks.

Parasites have frequently been labelled structurally 'degenerate', this could not be farther from the truth; how can a fluke with five or six distinct morphological phases, or a protozoan parasite like *Plasmodium* (the causative organism of malaria), having six structural forms, be rightly considered degenerate? Adult stages, from which this misconception has largely been formed, are the result of an unusual course of ecological specialization; to understand fully this line of specialization, it is necessary to compare the parasitic niche with that of a free living organism.

Free-living organisms must, of course, be fully adapted to the ecological demands of their niche. This usually includes some of the following: they must be able to move in order to avoid predators, hunt their prey, find a mate, etc.; to do this, limbs, fins, wings, and other organs of locomotion have been evolved. In order to coordinate their movements, many have developed structures sensitive to light, sound, heat, and chemicals. For control of movement and recognition of stimuli they are equipped with a complex nervous system, and have often developed intricate behavioural responses to the physical and chemical stimuli of the environment. Furthermore, the free-living organism must be able to reproduce and to carry on the basic requirements of life, while being structurally and physiologically modified to withstand the diverse fluctuations of its environment. The typical free-living organism will therefore be found, at all stages of its development, to be at least partially adapted to a large number of ecological demands.

In many instances certain tissues and organs have been developed to serve particular biological functions. The eye is adapted for seeing and similarly the leg for running. This illustrates a fundamental concept of biology that of 'division of labour', in which each organ or system performs a definite biological function, and is dependent on all the other organs and their functions as they are on it. Only the integrated organisms, the sum of the organic parts, is a viable and efficient individual entity. In the typical free-living organism it has been shown that a complete range of ecological adaptation is a minimum requirement for survival – but what of parasites?

Parasites also show a division of labour but in this case its development has been along different lines. The ecological division of labour, instead of concentrating itself into one stage or one level of organization, has become staggered throughout the life history. This has tended to produce a life-long division of labour where each particular biological demand is met with a distinct structural stage. Returning to the original theme of degeneracy, it may now be seen that many adult parasites are labelled degenerate when compared to free-living adults because their chief role in the parasite's life is propagation and, to a lesser extent, feeding.

In an attempt to illustrate the concept of a staggered division of labour, the life cycle of a common parasite will be briefly discussed. A typical fluke was mentioned above as having six

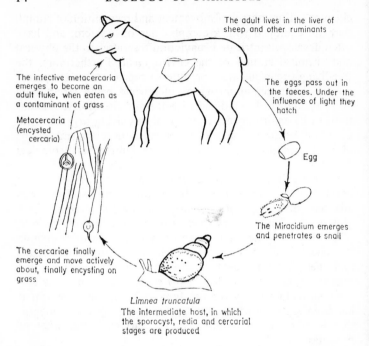

The adult lives in the liver of sheep and other ruminants

The infective metacercaria emerges to become an adult fluke, when eaten as a contaminant of grass

Metacercaria (encysted cercaria)

The eggs pass out in the faeces. Under the influence of light they hatch

Egg

The Miracidium emerges and penetrates a snail

The cercariae finally emerge and move actively about, finally encysting on grass

Limnea truncatula
The intermediate host, in which the sporocyst, redia and cercarial stages are produced

FIG. 3. The life cycle of the common fluke *Fasciola hepatica*

distinct morphological phases; by superimposing the concept of staggered division of labour, it may be seen that each stage is adapted to satisfy a particular ecological demand. *Fasciola hepatica*, the common liver fluke of sheep, may be taken as an example.

The adult, which lives in the bile duct, has a grossly developed reproductive system, and requires large amounts of food with which it forms enormous numbers of male and female gametes. The rest of its anatomy is simple; it has two suckers to maintain its position, a weak musculature for small movements and no

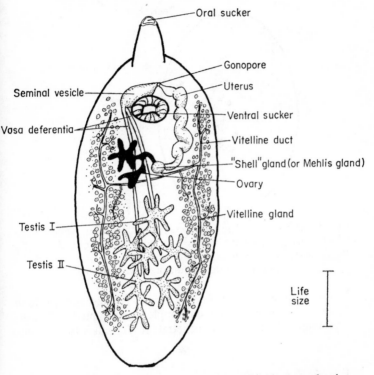

FIG. 4. The adult stage of *Fasciola hepatica*. Only the reproductive system is shown, and this is complex and highly developed.

specialized sense organs. Its only role in the biology of *Fasciola hepatica* is to propagate, and this it does effectively.

The products of this propagation stage are the eggs each containing a small embryo. The egg is a thick-walled, resistant, transport phase whose role it is to escape effectively from the host.

In the presence of light and water the egg hatches and a

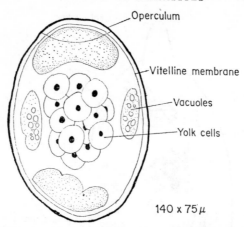

FIG. 5. The egg of *Fasciola hepatica*. A resistant walled stage which escapes from the host's bile duct to the outside world. Inside it are the developing primordia and the yolk cells for a supply of nutrients during development.

'miracidium' escapes to the free world. The biological role of the miracidium is singular and simple; it is adapted to find the snail intermediate host and penetrate it. To satisfy this purpose

FIG. 6. The miracidium of *Fasciola hepatica*. This phase must be motile and search out the next host, the snail *Limnaea trunctula*. Being a free-living phase in the life cycle it is equipped with eye-spots and cilia. It responds to light and there is also the suggestion that its behaviour is influenced by the snail's mucilage track.

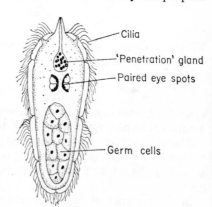

Redia

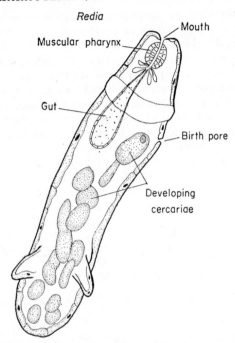

FIG. 7. The redia of *Fasciola hepatica*. The redial stage like the sporocyst stage is passed inside the snail, and is little more than a propagatory sac, it buds off cercariae from its inner wall and these emerge through the 'birth pore'.

it must be motile and sensitive to its environment. The miracidium, therefore, takes on a very different appearance from the adult, although both are *Fasciola hepatica*. The miracidium has a tapering streamlined body, and is covered with rapidly beating cilia; as a result, it is very active, moving at a considerable speed for its size. It is further modified by having eyes and showing chemoreception. The miracidium shows a definite positive phototaxis and there is evidence to suggest that it orientates itself to the mucilage stream of its snail host. On reaching the host, the miracidium is adapted to penetrate the snail integument by having an enzyme-secreting primitive gut.

Once inside the snail, the miracidium undergoes further morphological change and develops into the nearly structureless 'sporocyst' stage. The sporocyst and, later the redia, are asexual multiplication phases in the snail and they are not required to be motile nor to be sensitive to their surroundings. They have, therefore, no organs of locomotion or sensory apparatus.

The adaptations to this role, in the staggered division of labour of the parasite, are simple, and the sporocyst is little more than a propagatory sac, continually budding rediae from its internal cell lining. The redia, which is morphologically somewhat similar to the sporocyst, further increases the parasite's numbers by budding 'cercariae'.

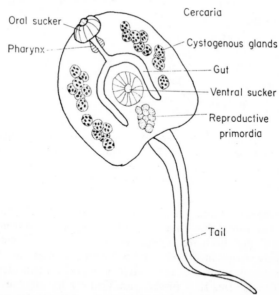

FIG. 8. The cercaria of *Fasciola hepatica*. The motile cercaria, after emergence from the snail swims to grass where it encysts becoming a metacercaria, which is infective to the definitive host.

The cercariae are not concerned with reproduction or feeding but, like the miracidia, only with transmission, this time returning to the sheep host. This they do by leaving the snail and swimming through the water, usually to herbage, on which they encyst, becoming infective 'metacercariae'.

The biological part played by the cercaria is, therefore, one of dispersal and transmission. As would be expected from the theme of this discussion, the cercaria is active and is modified by having a streamlined shape and a motile tail, its general appearance closely resembling that of a minute tadpole. The cercariae of some flukes also have eye spots.

After the cercaria encysts, the metacercaria is involved in the actual entry into the sheep; it is quiescent, non-feeding, resistant and long lived – features paralleled by the infective stages of many parasites. On being ingested by the host, the encapsulated metacercaria escapes from the cyst, partly by its own efforts, and bores its way into the abdominal cavity, and finally reaches the liver.

This very brief recapitulation of the *Fasciola hepatica* life cycle emphasizes the basic concept of a staggered division of labour.

Reproduction is performed sexually by the adult, and asexually by the sporocyst and redia, resistant stages are found in the egg and metacercaria, and motility is a feature of the miracidium and cercaria. All carry out basal metabolism, but each is adapted to play just one or two parts in the overall life of the liver fluke *Fasciola hepatica*.

It is hoped that the term 'degenerate', often levelled at parasites, will now be seen to be an incorrect description of a single highly adapted stage – the adult. The reproductive system of the adult is certainly not degenerate, it is instead extremely specialized; to relate the structure of the adult to its biological role is to display the adult not as degenerate but rather as highly modified. A common failing of the casual student is to forget that the egg, miracidium, sporocyst, redia, cercaria, metacercaria and adult are all phases in the composite biology of *Fasciola hepatica*.

The stages in a parasite's life cycle which are actually parasitic will become far more changed by their new environment than will those stages which disperse and transmit the parasite, the latter being justifiably considered free-living. Whereas the free-living stages of a parasite frequently retain the features of their free-living relatives, the parasitic stages become so extensively modified, that, following a short period of evolution, they may be unidentifiable with their free-living ancestors. It is for this reason that some taxonomists in parasitology search for the affinities of parasitic groups by studying the free-living stages, and not the grossly modified parasitic ones.

There are only a relatively few parasitic crustacea and most of these are bizarre, extravagantly developed egg sacs. For many years parasitologists were unable to identify these aberrant and largely amorphous parasites of fish, crabs, and other animals. The structure of the parasitic adults had become so fundamentally changed that it could not even be decided with certainty to which class of the arthropods they belonged. It is instructive to learn how in fact they were finally and accurately identified.

The parasitic adult of *Lernaeocera branchialis* for example, was identified by reference to its larval stages (Fig. 9). Different orders and superfamilies of crustacea are characterized by having their own peculiar larval stages, and the parasitic adults of *L. branchialis* give rise to larval free-living stages which are virtually indistinguishable from larvae of their free-living adult relatives. The biological role of the larvae has been unchanged although the adult has adopted parasitism. The staggered division of labour over the life cycle of the parasite has resulted in great changes in the parasitic stages, while hardly changing the free-living stages at all. The theme of differential specialization in the different ecological phases of the parasite's life is amply illustrated by a comparison of the larval and adult stages of the crustacean parasite *Lernaeocera branchialis* (Fig. 9).

When the characteristics of parasitic forms are discussed, it is useful to remember that often such characteristics are limited to the parasitic phases only. Among the parasitic phases certain

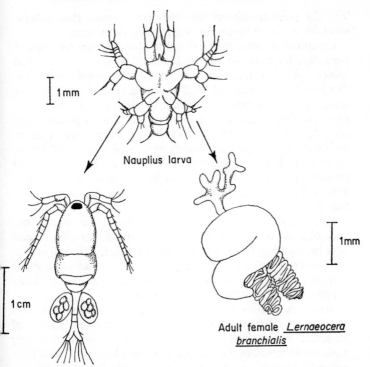

1 mm

Nauplius larva

1 mm

1 cm

Adult female *Lernaeocera*
branchialis

Adult female free-living
Copepod

Fig. 9. Morphological adaptations resulting from the parasitic habit have often led to the development of bizarre forms. The free-living phases however, which are still living as independent units have remained largely unchanged. This is illustrated by the grossly contrasting adult forms of a free-living adult copepod and the parasitic adult of *Lernaeocera branchialis*, while both share a similar planktonic larval stage—the Nauplius larva.

organs and structures are often lost and others modified. As has been shown above, the reproductive system is frequently highly developed, while the gut of some parasites has been completely lost, the parasites absorbing nutriment through their integument, as in the spiny-headed worms and tapeworms.

Certain structures, although not unique, are characteristic of parasites; for example, organs like hooks, claws, suckers, and spines (see Fig. 10). It is often essential for ectoparasites or gut-dwelling endoparasites to hold on to the skin or gut lining for temporary or permanent attachment. Many of these organs serve the dual purpose of holding the parasite in position and piercing the tissues. Hooks and suckers have been independently developed in such widely separated groups as flukes, tapeworms, leeches, spiny-headed worms, lice, fleas, mites, and parasitic crustaceans. Yet it must be remembered that hooks and suckers are also found among non-parasitic amphibians, fish and insects.

Parasitic stages are also characterized by the loss of locomotory organs. Biting lice, fleas, and other ectoparasitic insects may have greatly reduced wings and antennae, although retaining powerful legs for jumping; and endoparasites often move sluggishly with their reduced musculature. The overall body shape is typically flattened and elongated.

When zoologists attempt to study the relationships and affinities of different parasitic groups, the accepted features of structure, as characters of taxonomic importance, tend to lose their significance. In the comparative morphology of most non-parasitic groups, structural similarities are often used to indicate phylogenetic affinity; but in a study of parasites, structural similarities are frequently due to convergent evolution.

Many of the more conspicuous organs found in parasites are the consequence of their parasitic habit and do not relate to their ancestry. Spiny-headed worms and tapeworms both have an anteriorly placed organ armed with hooks; but this structural similarity is of little taxonomic worth, because the organ may be the result of parasitism and therefore be due to convergent evolution, and may not necessarily reflect any zoological affinity.

The solution of this problem is therefore very complex, for not only is there difficulty in finding a reliable taxonomic

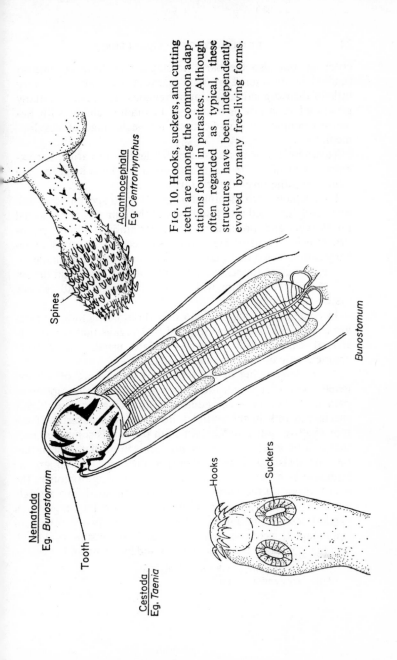

Acanthocephala
Eg. *Centrorhynchus*

Spines

Fig. 10. Hooks, suckers, and cutting teeth are among the common adaptations found in parasites. Although often regarded as typical, these structures have been independently evolved by many free-living forms.

Nematoda
Eg. *Bunostomum*

Tooth

Bunostomum

Cestoda
Eg. *Taenia*

Hooks

Suckers

criterion, but also the parasitic stages may have become so fundamentally altered by their parasitic existence, that very little of their orginal organization remains. The result, in many groups of parasites, is a state of taxonomic chaos, with numerous conflicting classifications for each stage of development.*

Taxonomic schemes exist which identify cercariae, for example, with no reference to and often no knowledge of the adults, and the reverse is also true.

Flukes have been identified at generic and specific level and tentatively grouped into families; but the affinities are reflected no further, and no satisfactory superfamilies, suborders, or orders exist. Parasitic creatures have become so morphologically camouflaged that many are taxonomically quite unidentifiable, and often the schemes available are artificial and do not reflect true relationships which are the purpose of all genuine systematic schemes.

In conclusion it may be said that certain structural features are characteristic of parasites, and that organs that are loosely termed characteristic of parasites are usually more truly characteristic of parasitic stages.

An understanding of the ecological significance of a 'staggered division of labour' helps to remove the misconception of parasitic degeneracy, the adult parasite being a single, highly specialized link in the complex life cycle of a parasite. If the reproductive system of a gravid adult parasite is compared with that of a typical free-living creature, it is immediately seen that the parasite is at a higher level of specialization. To compare the structure of a parasite with that of a free-living organism, the sum total of all the parasitic stages concentrated into a single composite organism must be compared with the stages of a single free-living individual.† Just as the free-living individual is a complete, ecologically viable animal, so the sum total of all a parasite's stages is an ecologically independent unit.

* This applies more usually to endoparasites.
† Or a larva and an adult.

3

Parasitism—The Ecological Niche

MANY aspects of parasitism are so unusual that the layman or casual student is inclined to think of the parasitic niche as something almost unnatural. The phenomenon of one animal living inside or on another animal is fundamentally difficult to accept as just another form of life.

Medical and veterinary textbooks tend to emphasize the morbid aspects of parasitism and this correlation of parasitism with disease has tended to discredit parasitism as an ecological niche. In reality the relationship between host and parasite is a truly ecological one.

There is nothing sinister or macabre about parasites, and although the niche is unusual, it is by no means unnatural. Parasitism is an essential part of any natural community and the parasite is far less a hazard to its host than is a predator to its prey. The adaptations of the host to withstand parasitic infection are no less important than the host's adaptations to overcome cold or fatigue. Parasites do not by any means 'have it all their own way' and, in their free-living stages alone, must overcome great ecological hazards. The extent of the hazards is illustrated by the enormous number of eggs some parasites must lay to ensure the survival of their kind, for example *Ascaris* which can lay 100,000 per day.

Parasites have evolved to become an essential factor in the equilibrium of a natural community. They exercise a degree of natural control which is of long-standing biological importance, and are present in any natural population.

The well-adapted parasite must be able both to exploit the advantages and to withstand the hazards of its niche.

One of the most important advantages of parasitism must be

the constant and unlimited food supply which a host supplies. Gut dwellers get a meal every time the host feeds, and probably more often than that; and blood or tissue feeders have a continual supply of food as long as the host remains healthy. The advantage is further increased by the actual nature of the food. Living in the gut or tissues of the host, or feeding ectoparasitically on blood, may render unnecessary a complex digestive enzyme system, as the food is pre-digested by the host, and moves about the host's body as simple carbohydrates, fats and amino acids, which can be directly assimilated by the parasite. The parasite enjoys, therefore, an abundant supply of food of a basically simple nature and, equally important, this food is in close proximity, demanding little or no movement on behalf of the parasite.

Once established in or on a host, the parasite is carried passively wherever the host may chance to wander. This ensures a passive distribution of the parasite's eggs and infective stages. Looking slightly deeper into the ecological consequences of this, it means that a concentration of hosts will lead to a concentration of parasites, thereby increasing the likelihood of successful transmission. This applies not only to the local movements but also to the larger scale migrations of the hosts, and ensures even inter-continental distribution for the parasites of migrating birds and mammals – a considerable achievement for a parasite that may be under a millimetre long!

Another major advantage of the parasitic existence, at least in parasites of vertebrates, particularly those which are warm-blooded, is the assurance of a constant environment. Although the microhabitat of the parasite may demand considerable specialization, once a parasite has become sufficiently adapted it is guaranteed independence from the fluctuations of the external conditions. This constancy is of paramount importance to the parasite, as it allows the continual production of eggs, independent of seasonal control or environmental fluctuation, an advantage shared by very few non-parasitic creatures.

The host also affords protection from predators, and such physical factors as radiation, drought, and flood; although it must be remembered that many of these advantages apply more strictly to endoparasites than to ectoparasites.

A few of the major ecological advantages of parasitism have been discussed, but there are also major disadvantages.

Firstly, there is the host-reaction to the parasite's intrusion. The host has an extensive range of defence mechanisms to fight the intruder; these range from the direct physical protection of skin, to the more biochemical aspects of inflammation, immunity, and calcareous cyst formation. These host reactions are dealt with more fully in the chapter on host–parasite relationships, but they are directly relevant here, and any successful parasite must be adequately adapted to withstand the whole extent of the host reaction.

There is also the direct problem of the physical hazard encountered when living in or on another animal. For ectoparasites, which are often blood feeders, there is the necessity for a piercing and sucking apparatus and, whenever possible, they must be able to avoid the scratching or biting behaviour of the host. It is not surprising that concentrations of ectoparasites are found on the back of the head of voles and mice, the one position where the host cannot scratch effectively.

Endoparasites have an even more precarious existence; if they enter through the mouth (as the majority do), they must withstand the mastication. If they pass beyond this, they must successfully oppose the crushing action imposed by those hosts with gizzards, the corrosive gastric secretions and the continual peristalsis churning the gut contents along its whole length. It is a common misconception that a tapeworm, for example, hangs limp in the gut of its host – in fact it is for ever writhing and twisting 'against the current', by gross muscular contractions. If a mouse or bird with a tapeworm infection is killed and the abdominal cavity immediately opened, the intestine is a heaving mass of tapeworms, which actively move about in a dish of water if given the opportunity.

The suckers and hooks of such familiar endoparasites as flukes tend to imply that the parasite is permanently fixed, it is, however, becoming increasingly obvious that this is not so, the suckers and hooks are used more for a temporary hold in leech-like movements as they wander through the gut.

Once a parasite has managed to pass the teeth (and perhaps gizzard) and has tolerated the churning of the host's peristalsis, and fought sufficiently vigorously against the through current of the gut contents, it has to withstand the physical and bio-chemical hazards of its microhabitat. As a foreign protein in the gut, it is greatly in danger of being digested. A problem which it must overcome. It must further be able to tolerate the drastic changes which characterize different regions of the alimentary canal.

Superimposed on all these problems is the parasite's 'per-sonal' problem of hatching (if it entered in an egg or in a cyst), and ending up in the right region of the host's body. Few para-sites are found in more than one region or tissue, and it is to this site only that they are fully adapted.

While still reviewing the problems of life within a host, the problem of escape may be mentioned (see Fig. 11). Parasites are to be found in every major tissue or organ-system of the body, and yet their eggs or infective stages must be able to escape from these organs, which are often deep-seated, to the outside world. This is the first hurdle in transmission for the parasite, and many fascinating adaptations are found to over-come it. As the parasite inhabits such a specialized ecological niche, it could only survive with bizarre adaptations. Parasites are so modified that they depend more and more on exploiting the biology of their hosts for transmission and less on their own structure or physiology. What they lack in structural adapt-ability they compensate for in ingenuity! There are five main routes of exit which endoparasites use to escape from their vertebrate hosts and in most cases the one used corresponds to the site of parasitization.

Gut dwellers have no great problem, for their eggs and juvenile stages may easily pass out in the excreta. There is one particular stomach-dwelling nematode of cats which does not, however, use this route. Infective stages of the nematode *Ollulanus tricuspis*, pass out in the vomit of the cat (a normal feature of the cat's biology), and it is thought that they are transmitted when the vomit is licked by another cat (Cameron).

As parasites venture from the gut to deeper tissues, the difficulty of escape becomes increasingly more complex. Lung dwellers use the faecal route almost exclusively although, as might be expected, some parasitic stages pass out in the sputum during coughing. In this case the parasite is exploiting the coughing habit of its host, or is passed passively up the trachea by the host's cilia, followed by the swallowing reflex, which carries it into the gut.

The liver is another organ which is parasitized by a wide range of organisms, and not all use the same mode of escape. The bile duct connects the liver with the intestine, so that some parasites enter and leave the liver by this convenient duct. The liver is also in direct connection with the intestine via the hepatic portal system, and many parasites, usually the smaller ones, use this route although the blood current flows from the intestine to the liver. The fine structure of the liver also provides another obstacle to escape; only certain parts are in direct communication with the bile duct, the others being at a 'dead end'; the nematode parasite *Capillaria hepatica* is in such a predicament. In the liver, the female of the species lays eggs continually and these may be seen as long yellow strands, the eggs are, however, trapped having no direct communication with the outside. In this case the 'release mechanism' comes at the death of the host. *Capillaria hepatica* is found in the liver of rabbits and if the rabbit is devoured by a predator, any predator, the eggs pass through its gut and end up in the outside world. As far as is known, the predator offers no more than release to the parasite. This method of escape is completely passive on the part of the parasite, depending entirely on the biology of its host and the host's predators.

The blood provides further difficulties to the many parasites that are found in it. With the notable exception of the medically important blood fluke, *Schistosoma*, blood-dwelling parasites do not use the anal route of escape.

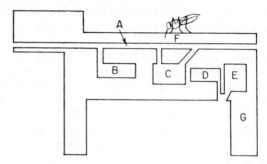

FIG. 11. The exit and entry of parasites of a generalized vertebrate host.

A. *Alimentary tract.* The parasites of this organ system generally enter orally and escape via the rectal route. As the alimentary tract occupies such a central position it is also used by the parasites on other organs.

B. *Lungs.* The parasites of the lungs enter orally or actively penetrate the skin reaching the lungs via the pulmonary circulation. They leave by being wafted up the trachea by ciliary tracts and swallowed or being coughed in the sputum.

C. *Liver.* The liver has connections with the circulatory system and is connected to the gut by the bile duct and indirectly by the hepatic portal system. Being large, central and rich in food reserves, the liver has been exploited by many parasites. They gain entry and exist by one of the routes mentioned.

D & E. *The urino-genital complex.* Parasites of these organ systems may enter orally and migrate from the gut, but exit is usually via the urinary route. It is from this organ complex that parasites transmitted during coition are found.

F. *The skin.* Entry by active penetration, and entry and exit by inoculation through a blood sucking vector is the method used by many of the important parasites of the circulatory system and connective tissues.

G. *Muscle tissue.* Encystment or encapsulation in deep-seated tissues represents a biological *cul-de-sac*. Transmission or escape in this case can only be affected through the host falling prey to another host and the parasite being released (see also Fig. 12).

It is more characteristic to employ the services of an inter-mediate host, commonly a blood-feeding ectoparasite. Ticks, fleas, reduvid bugs, tabanid flies, and Pupipara are all involved in the transmission of blood parasites. Leeches have also been implicated and even the blood-feeding vampire bats are thought to be involved in the transmission of a blood-parasitic proto-zoan in South America.

In the majority of cases, the blood-feeding intermediate host not only makes the escape possible, but is also concerned in the further inoculation of a new host.

It may be stressed here that such intermediate hosts, or vectors as they are commonly called, are themselves parasitized and it is incorrect, for example, to think of the mosquito which transmits the malarial parasite, as being 'on the side of the parasite'.

Some parasites live in the host's musculature, and what is more, they are very often in capsules, being completely unable to move – such a parasite is the trichina worm *Trichinella spiralis*. The only escape mechanism in this case comes when the host muscle is eaten (see Fig. 12). It is understandable, therefore, that the natural host of this parasite is the rat – an animal frequently practising cannibalism. Pigs, from which man occasionally becomes infected with this worm, pick up the infection from eating the remains of dead rats (see also the chapter on transmission).

The guinea worm *Dracunculus medinensis*, the females of which are up to a metre long and migrate through man's con-nective tissue, produce larval stages. The gravid female moves to the legs or arms of the infected individual and produces a hot blister or cyst just under the skin. The normal reaction to this is for the host to bathe the inflamed area, causing the blister to burst and myriads of larvae to pass into the water. This is a case of a connective tissue parasite which can move and does not depend on a blood-sucking vector.

The urinary system is another major means of escape from the host. As the system is itself morphologically planned to serve the dual function of reproduction and nitrogenous

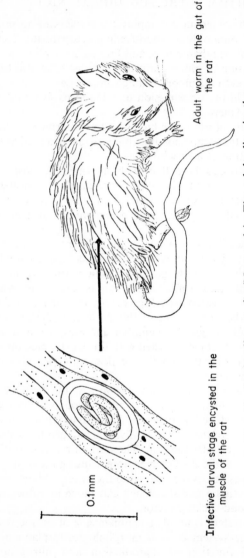

Infective larval stage encysted in the muscle of the rat

0.1mm

Adult worm in the gut of the rat

FIG. 12. *Trichinella spiralis* (Nematoda). The adults live in the gut but the infective larval stages become encysted in the muscles of rats (and other mammals). The natural transmission depends on the cannibalism of the rats.

excretion, it is largely the parasites of these organ systems that use the urinary route of escape. There are some blood parasites also (e.g. *Schistosoma haematobium*) in which the eggs pass into the host's bladder from the bloodstream and are carried out passively in the urine.

Allied to the urinary route is the sexual path of escape which is discussed further in the next chapter, a few highly adapted parasites being passed in host coition.

The last, and possibly most interesting form of escape is ovarian or hereditary transmission. This is discussed further in the following chapter, and includes examples of parasites which infect the young of their hosts '*in utero*' or pass to the developing eggs of the host.

Following directly on the problem of escape is the problem of transmission, or re-entry: this will be dealt with more fully in the next chapter.

Another biological hazard of the parasitic way of life is that of finding a mate. It will be appreciated by now that the likelihood of successful transmission is very small, and once transmitted that of finding a mate may be even more remote. Apart from the mere statistical improbability of finding a mate, there is also the topographical problem. If two blood parasitic worms – a male and a female – reach the same host, let us say an elephant, and neither worm is much more than a fraction of an inch long, it will be agreed that their difficulties are far from being solved!

Parasites have evolved many ingenious solutions to this problem, not least the obvious one of hermaphroditism (Fig. 13). Although not unique to parasites, hermaphroditism is often one of their characteristics, the best known examples being among the flatworms, the flukes and tapeworms.

Another solution, although not usually given this interpretation, is the habit of asexual larval multiplication frequently found among parasites. This habit has the direct advantage resulting from an increase in numbers, while giving the possibility of an *increase* without the necessity for sexual differentiation.

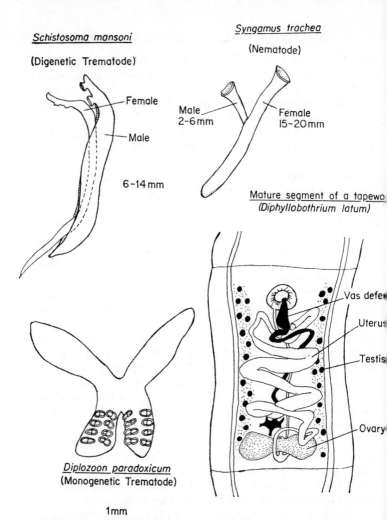

Schistosoma mansoni

(Digenetic Trematode)

Female
Male
6-14 mm

Syngamus trachea

(Nematode)

Male
2-6mm
Female
15-20mm

Mature segment of a tapewo
(*Diphyllobothrium latum*)

Vas defe
Uterus
Testis
Ovary

Diplozoon paradoxicum
(Monogenetic Trematode)

1mm

FIG. 13. One of the problems facing dioecious parasites (separate males and females) is that of finding and remaining with a mate. The figure shows some of the ways in which the problem is overcome, including the widespread phenomenon of hermaphroditism characteristic of flukes and tapeworms.

Cyst formation, a parasite provoked host-reaction, can be another answer to the problem of finding a mate – although not a common one. An aberrant annelid parasite *Myzostomum*, common on the feather star (*Antedon bifida*) in the lower zones of the seashore, is found in little cysts between the axials of the crinoids' arms. If these cysts are opened, two parasites may be found, a male and a female, living together.

Similarly, a nematode parasite (*Cystoopsis acipenseri*), on the skin of the sturgeon, is found in cysts containing a male and a female. In both these examples, if one may be teleological, the partners have met and, to ensure that they stay together, have either constructed their own cyst or caused the host to produce a cyst around them. This adaptation is one solution to the problem of keeping a mate.

A rather unusual phenomenon of cyst formation is found in one family of flukes (Troglotrematidae). The lung fluke, *Paragonimus westermani*, is found in small brown cysts in the lungs. In each cyst there are two hermaphroditic animals but, in this case, the tendency is towards separate sexes, one of the partners having a better developed male reproductive system and the other a better female system. This tendency is no doubt favoured by evolutionary selective forces, as it ensures a greater genetical mixture, always thought to be an advantage to the race.

This example may be thought of as the result first of hermaphroditism and, secondly of cyst partnership, the hermaphroditic habit being superseded on cyst formation.

The gapeworm, *Syngamus trachea*, a parasite economically important in poultry farming, lives in the trachea of chickens. It is of a unique form, having the over-all shape of the letter 'Y' (see Fig. 13). One of the arms of the Y is, in fact, the male, the rest being the female. The male is permanently fused to the female and thereby overcomes the problem of finding a mate. This example also demonstrates the tendency to reduction in the size of the male, a frequent consequence of permanent fusion. *Diplozoon paradoxicum*, a monogenetic tremotode found on the gills of fishes (Fig. 13) cannot develop to maturity until it finds a partner, with which it fuses.

Among the nematodes may also be found examples of three other ways of overcoming the problem. One of the most unusual is that of *Trichosomoides crassicauda*, which occurs in the bladder of the rat. The male *Trichosomoides crassicauda* is minute and lives as a hyperparasite in the vulva of the female, its only biological function is the production of male gametes and so it lives its whole life inside the female.

Parthenogenesis is a solution one might expect to find more frequently than is actually the case, though some animal parasitic nematodes are, in fact, parthenogenetic. One very unusual solution is that of 'syngony', really a form of extreme protandrous hermaphroditism – in which the parasite is first a functional male and then after storage of its own gametes, becomes a functional female, finally fertilizing its own eggs with its own spermatozoa.

There are other ecological hazards of parasitism including the all important problem of transmission. One of the 'far-sighted' adaptations of parasites are those which prevent excess damage being done to their hosts – parasites must live on interest and not on capital. Disease of the host is usually a result of hyperinfestation rather than the effect of individual parasites. There are found in the biology of parasites, adaptations at individual and population levels, which tend to avoid disease of the host by parasitic hyperinfestation (see Chapter 9).

Following a brief review of the ecology of parasitism, it may be appreciated that parasites are controlled by environmental factors which are both advantageous and disadvantageous, and they fit into the equilibrium of a natural community.

All that has been said so far concerns the immediate surroundings of the parasite, the microenvironment. Dogiel and other Russian authors have also emphasized the importance of the macroenvironment, or the environment of the host, in relation to the parasitic burden. In periods when the external environment fluctuates, parasites may also be affected, this has been shown, for example, during host hibernation.

Many years ago Heitz (1918) in an inspired piece of work, recorded the parasites of migrating salmon at the mouth of the river Rhine, repeating his records at intervals up the river. He found that on entering fresh water the salmon lost their marine parasites, and that these were quickly replaced by fresh water species. Similar data exist for the eel which migrates from fresh water to the sea.

The macroenvironment can, therefore, have a direct influence on the parasitic fauna, or it may act indirectly through the host.

A successful parasite must be able to withstand the hazards and exploit the benefits of its niche, while at the same time preserving the health of its host.

4

Transmission

ONE of the less obvious characteristics of parasitism, and yet one of fundamental importance, is the inclusion in the life cycle of a stage independent of its host. A stage is reached in the life cycle of almost all parasites, when they cannot develop further in or on the definitive host, for example, both eggs and many protozoan oocysts develop only in an aerobic environment and so must pass to the outside before continuing their development.

This feature in the life of parasites has two immediate advantages: firstly, it permits dispersal of infective stages and is, therefore, essential for the continued infection of new hosts; secondly, it may be interpreted as a safety device on the part of the parasite, which tends to avoid hyperinfestation of the host. If the enormous numbers of eggs laid by the adults were all to develop inside the same individual host, disease and death of the host would be inevitable.

The essential period of existence independent of the definitive host may, therefore, be seen to have definite biological advantages; it does, however, create a major problem in the ecology of parasitism. Once a parasite has embarked on this period of isolation it loses contact with its host. As a result much of the biology of the transmitting stages is directed exclusively at regaining entry into another host. It was stated above that a stage is reached in which the parasite can only develop further when independent of the host. Similarly, during transmission, a stage is reached where development can only continue on finding another host.

Because of the biological significance of this period of hazard, adaptations are found not only in the transmitting stages themselves, but also in the adults, which enhance the likelihood of successful transmission. Adults are modified to lay astronomical numbers of eggs and larvae, often up to millions per day. The vast egg production may be considered as a numerical adaptation to compensate for the very high mortality rate suffered during transmission.

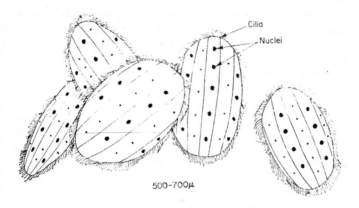

FIG. 14 *Opalina ranarum* (Protozoa). An almost universal parasite of frogs, occurring in the hind gut and just discernable with the unaided eye. This parasite has restricted its breeding period to coincide with that of its host.

It is a feature of successful parasites that they must show extensive specialization and adaptation to their hosts. They must be adapted biochemically, physiologically, and structurally, but in this chapter the ecological adaptations will be considered. Just as parasites are adapted biochemically to withstand, for example, the host immunity response, so they are adapted ecologically to gain access to their hosts.

As in all host–parasite relationships, parasites have become highly modified ecologically in conformation to the biology of their own particular hosts. Often the feeding habits of the hosts are *exploited by* parasites which enter by the mouth. Other parasites are closely adapted to different biological events in the lives of their hosts; these include: feeding, migration, breeding, and moulting as well as the more specific biology of individual hosts. In all these cases the peculiar parasitic fauna of each host has become ecologically adapted to the host's habits and depends on them for successful transmission (see Fig. 12 and others).

The process of transmission includes all the events between escaping from one host and re-infecting the same host species again; it therefore covers the whole of the life cycle from one adult parasite to the next. In this general context transmission may or may not incorporate an intermediate host, and the free-living stages may be motile or may be transferred passively in a cyst or egg from one host to the next.

In an attempt to illustrate this principle a few of the main methods employed by parasites for successful transmission will be given. Examples are included which show how parasites exploit the particular biology of their own hosts.

Chronological adaptations

1. Hosts often have limited reproductive periods and a number of parasites have restricted their own propagative efforts to coincide with the host's breeding cycles. Such an adaptation may be coordinated by many different factors but there is evidence to show that in some cases the parasite is under the direct hormonal control of the host (Fig. 2).

In some parasites this restricted breeding period is an ecological necessity, as, for example, in *Polystomum integerrimum* (Fig. 15), and the protozoan *Opalina ranarum* (Fig. 14), both parasites of the frog. The host in this case has a breeding cycle for only a limited time in the year and at this time the adult frogs, their spawn and the tadpoles are all strictly aquatic.

The infective stages of both these parasites depend on an aquatic medium and, therefore, they can only breed during this restricted period. *Opalina* and *Polystoma* infect the frog at the

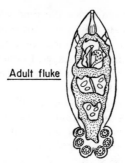

Adult fluke

↕ Life size

Life cycle

FIG. 15. *Polystomum integerrimum.* (Monogenea Trematoda.) *Polystomum* occurs in the bladder of frogs and like *Opalina* (Fig. 14) has restricted and synchronized its reproductive effort with that of its host.

tadpole stage. This habit may be an evolutionary remnant from a time when the amphibian was more wholly aquatic and, as the host became emancipated, taking up the terrestrial habit, its parasites were compelled to restrict their breeding times to the limited periods of aquatic existence. The result has been that the host and its parasites synchronize their breeding times to the host's aquatic stage.

Restricting the breeding period to coincide with the host's breeding period has two overall ecological advantages for the parasite. It reserves its propagative effort for the short period of host concentration, and for the time when there are many young susceptible hosts. The concentration of adults is probably more important as a source of infection, supplying a sufficient number of infective stages, to contaminate the young stages. The juveniles, with their low resistance, are subjected to a high infection rate at this time.

Haemonchus contortus, an economically important nematode of sheep, increase its egg output in the spring; this coincides with the lambing period and again synchronizes with the concentration of hosts and the presence of young. This phenomenon is known as the 'spring rise', and is a widespread phenomenon among ruminant parasites.

The flagellate *Trichonympha*, symbiotic in the intestine of wood-eating insects (see Fig. 2), has a reproductive phase which is synchronized with the moulting of its host. This is an ecological necessity and is under the control of a host moulting hormone.

2. There are also daily periodicities in some blood parasites, coinciding with the periodic feeding habits of their blood-sucking transmitting hosts (see Fig. 16).

There is a group of nematodes, the filarial worms, which live in the blood, lymph, and connective tissue of vertebrates, including man. The embryonated pre-larval stages or 'microfilariae' swim freely in the host's blood and lymph and are transmitted by blood-sucking insects, being accidentally taken up in the blood meal. Experiments have shown that the microfilariae are chemotactically attracted to the insects' salivary secretion. In addition to this adaptation, another peculiarity of a few species of microfilariae is their nocturnal or diurnal periodicity. As an illustration of this periodicity, two filarial worms of medical importance will be discussed : *Wuchereria bancrofti*, the causative organism of the dramatic filarial elephantiasis, and *Loa loa*, the 'eye worm' of West and Central Africa.

The adults of *Wuchereria bancrofti* inhabit the ducts and nodes of the lymphatic system of man. They break down the valves of the vessels and form reservoirs of lymph which cause the grotesque symptoms of elephantiasis. The adult worms mate in the lymph ducts and eggs are laid from which microfilariae are formed. The microfilariae migrate through the lymph ducts and into the host's blood system.

During the daytime the microfilariae concentrate in the capillaries of the lungs but, between 10 p.m. and 4 a.m., they are found in greatest concentration in the peripheral blood. The actual mechanism or control of this periodicity is still a matter of controversy (Hawking, 1965), but for transmission of the parasite, the phenomenon is ideal. The intermediate hosts of *Wuchereria bancrofti* in Africa are various species of *Culex*, *Aedes*, and *Anopheles* (mosquitoes), which are nocturnal feeders. The result of the microfilarial periodicity is that the greatest concentration of parasites is in the peripheral blood at the time that the vector is feeding. In this example both the positive chemotactic behaviour of the microfilaria to the mosquito's salivary secretion, and the nocturnal period-icity increase the likelihood of successful transmission (see Fig. 16).

In some Pacific islands there is no periodicity of *W. bancrofti* microfilariae and the intermediate hosts are not nocturnal feeders. (For the latest review on microfilarial periodicity see Hawking 1965.)

Loa loa the 'eye worm', is found mainly in the subcutaneous connective tissue of man and monkeys. In man the adults migrate through the subcutaneous tissue and often chance to cross the eye-ball, under the conjunctiva – it is this habit that has given *Loa loa* its popular name.

Unlike *Wuchereria bancrofti*, the microfilariae of *Loa loa* show an opposite periodicity, being in the peripheral blood in greatest numbers during the daytime, and almost disappearing from the blood at night. This reversed periodicity, however, correlates perfectly with the contrasting feeding habits of the intermediate host. The insect which transmits *Loa loa*, is a diurnally feeding tabanid fly known as the Mangrove fly, *Chrysops*.

Periodicity is, therefore, another chronological adaptation

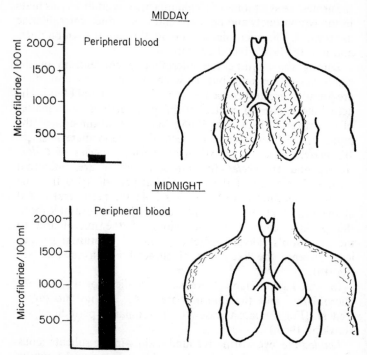

FIG. 16. Microfilarial periodicity of *Wuchereria bancrofti*. During the daytime the microfilariae are held in the lungs by a 'retention factor' which is not operative, or below its threshold at night. It has been suggested that the periodicity is related to a circadian rhythm in the host, and oxygen tension has been implicated. The biological advantage is that the microfilariae are present in the peripheral blood at the same time that the mosquito vector is feeding.

to aid in the success of transmission; in the particular case of microfilariae, the periodicity may be thought of as an elaborate adaptation to escape from the host. It is an ecological adaptation to the feeding behaviour of the transmitting insect. It seems possible that these movements of the microfilariae may be governed by the rhythmic dilation and contraction of the host blood vessels, over a 24-hour period.

3. There are many other examples of adaptations concerned with time or periodicity, e.g. in the guinea worm *Dracunculus medinensis*. This nematode has its larval stages in the copepods which swim in the wells and lakes of Africa. The infection is transmitted to man when he drinks water containing copepods carrying infective larvae.

If a copepod becomes infected, it drops to the bottom of the well; this stage in the annual cycle of the parasite coinciding with the period of drought. The result of this time adaptation, is to increase the probability of infection by concentrating the infective larvae in a small volume of water.

Behaviour of the host

Essentially, all adaptations for transmission exploit some aspect of the host's behaviour, be it feeding habits, migratory habits or some other behavioural trait. This section, however, is aimed more particularly at the unique or unusual biological habits of certain hosts, which are exploited by their own parasitic fauna.

For example, the grey seal (*Halichoerous grypus*) has a peculiar habit of rubbing its nose against that of other seals as a sign of recognition. It is thought that it is during this act that the hydracarinid mite, parasitic in the seal's nasal chambers, is transmitted from one seal to the next. The mite is completely dependent for its continued survival on this particular behavioural character of its host.

One of the parasitic flukes of frogs, *Diplodiscus*, lives as an adult in the hind gut of the frog and passes its larval stage in a snail. The infective larval stage of *Diplodiscus*, having emerged from the snail, encysts as a metacercaria in the skin of frogs and tadpoles showing a preference for dark spots. Adult frogs become infected when eating the moulted skin of the stratum corneum, containing the metacercariae. Tadpoles pick up the metacercariae along with the respiratory stream of water.

Perhaps the most basic of all biological functions, not restricted to any one group, is sexual behaviour. A few parasites have become dependent on the sex act for their transmission, one of the best known being the spirochaetes which cause syphilis and other venereal diseases of man. This method of transmission is not restricted to mankind, among other examples are parasites of horses and cattle. *Trypanosoma equiperdum*, a member of the genus discussed more fully in Chapter 7, is transmitted during coition in horses. *Trichomonas vaginalis*, another protozoan, this time parasitic in cattle, causes 'still-birth' in some cases, and is transmitted during coition.

From the overall standpoint of transmission, infection through the sex act, by direct and immediate contact between two hosts *of the same species*, creates a fundamental problem. It is perhaps of only academic interest, but such a mode of transmission throws a slight doubt on the generalized statement that parasites must have a period of independent existence between hosts. Fundamentally, the parasite must pass from one individual to another and, by definition, from one sex to another, but free-living existence as such is doubtful.

Hereditary transmission

One of the most interesting adaptations for transmission has been independently developed by distantly related parasitic groups; it is that of directly infecting the eggs or larvae of the host.

One of the most extensively studied examples of 'transovarian transmission' is that of the piroplasm *Babesia bigemina* (see Fig. 17). This minute protozoan parasite is transmitted by the blood-sucking tick *Boophilus*. *Babesia bigemina* causes the disease 'Red water fever' or haemoglobinuric fever, both names referring to the chief symptom, that of the cattle hosts passing

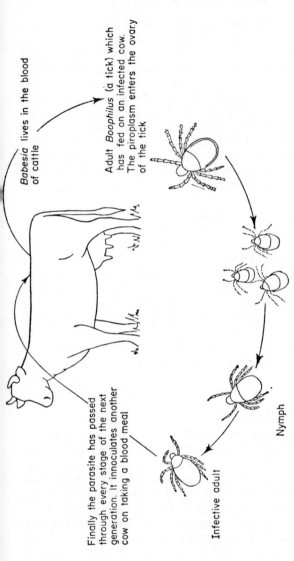

Babesia lives in the blood of cattle

Adult Boophilus (a tick) which has fed on an infected cow. The piroplasm enters the ovary of the tick

The next generation larvae are born, carrying the infection

Nymph

Infective adult

Finally the parasite has passed through every stage of the next generation. It innoculates another cow on taking a blood meal

FIG. 17. The life cycle of Babesia bigemina (Piroplasm, Protozoa). The transmission depends on the parasite passing through the gut of the tick and infecting the ovaries. The ticks of the next generation infect cattle when they take a blood meal.

red urine owing to haemoglobin breakdown by the parasite. The tick which transmits *Babesia* has only one blood meal in its life, and then produces young and does not return to blood feeding. The effect of this on the biology of the parasite is to create an ecological 'cul de sac'. Only one way out is available to the parasite for its continuation and that is the route actually taken. Very small larval stages of *Babesia*, merozoites, migrate to the tick's ovaries and enter the eggs and developing larvae of the tick, thereby infecting the next generation. When, after metamorphosis, the young adult sucks the blood of another bovine host, it is responsible for inoculating the parasite; *Babesia* itself having passed through intermediate hosts, the parent and the daughter ticks.

There is evidence to suggest that some parasites are transmitted from mother to embryo in placental mammals. To achieve infection 'in utero', a parasitic stage must be very small and have access to the bloodstream; a nematode *Toxacara canis*, found in dogs, can be transmitted in this way. Both ovarian and uterine transmission ensure the infection of the correct species of host, directly, and with the minimum amount of hazard. It is perhaps surprising that this method of transmission is not more common, but it must be remembered that the morphological and physiological placental barrier, is extensively adapted to withstand this kind of invasion.

Behaviour of the parasites

The majority of parasites include in their life cycle, not only an independent stage but an independent free-living stage. It is the purpose of this stage to disperse the parasite and to make contact with the next host. In many cases, this infective organism is encysted or encapsulated and depends completely on the habits of the potential host, or on the effect of the elements for its passive transmission. There are infective stages, however, that are responsive to the physical and chemical stimuli of their surroundings, and these have taxes and kineses, as well as characteristic behavioural responses which enhance their chance of finding a host.

Investigation into the behaviour of the free-living infective stages is still in its infancy, but what is known is of considerable interest (Wallace, 1961). Experiment has shown that certain miracidia (the first larval stages of flukes) whose role in life it is to penetrate a snail, are chemically attracted to the mucus secretion of the snail. The actively penetrating cercaria of the medically important blood fluke, *Schistosoma*, which penetrates into the skin when feet or hands are submerged in water, has characteristic behaviour patterns. These infective stages, and others, are activated by shadows or, more exactly, by a sudden change in light intensity, which may inform them of the whereabouts of potential hosts.

Hookworm larvae of *Ancylostoma duodenale* which actively penetrate into the skin of man, are attracted by heat, and are thought to be negatively geotactic. Both these taxes enhance the probability of successful transmission. Some nematodes are activated by light, the response varying with the intensity; at dawn and dusk the light intensity is at an optimum and it is at that time that they are most active.

It is the role of many free-living stages to be devoured by an intermediate host, and a number of adaptations have been found which would appear to be directed to this end. There is a group of worms, parasitic as adults in vertebrates, the spiny-headed worms or Acanthocephala, whose eggs pass out in the droppings; these eggs are then devoured by copepods. Some authorities (Scheuring) believe that these eggs resemble the diatoms which are the copepods' normal food, thereby 'camouflaging' the parasite egg to look like a diatom.

Among the cercariae which are devoured by fish, and then encyst inside them, is the cercaria of the fluke *Azygia*. As an adaptation to make the cercaria look conspicuous, it twists and bends its body continually, drawing the attention of its favoured predator and mimicking the movements of midge larvae which are the fishes' natural foodstuff.

The principle illustrated by *Azygia*, that of 'drawing attention to itself", is not unusual and is one of the most important fields of adaptation for transmission. There is a fluke, parasitic in some birds, which depends for its survival on one of these birds eating a snail inside which the young stage of the fluke is developing. The sporocyst stage of the fluke *Leucochloridium paradoxum* branches and grows all through the tissues; finally it produces two sacs and these sacs grow out into the tentacles of the snail, *Succinea*. They cause the tentacles to pulsate at rates of 50–100 times per minute (depending on temperature), and look like two Belisha beacons (Wesenberg-Lund, 1931). In addition to this, the parasite has a 'psychological' effect on the snail and the snail develops an affinity for light, moving to the edge of the leaves on which it lives, and so putting itself in full view of any passing bird.

The parasite, in these examples, has a definite and often profound effect on the behaviour and appearance of its host, the result being to isolate the host from other members of the same species and make it attractive to the next host.

There are authors (for review see Wallace, 1963) who believe the potato root eelworm *Heterodera rostochiensis*, to be chemically attracted by the exudate of its plant host. Workers in this field have even gone as far as to isolate the chemotactic attractant and have named it, eclepic acid.

Another fluke, *Cryptocotyle lingua*, parasitic as an adult in gulls and terns, is commonly found in the seashore birds of Britain. The eggs are passed in the droppings of the bird and are picked up by *Littorina littorea* (the edible winkle)* (see Fig. 18). The cercariae later come out of the winkle and in May and June penetrate into herrings and other shore fish. When the infected herrings are eaten by the gulls, the adult stage is reached and the life cycle is completed (see Fig. 18).

Littorina littorea is normally found in only one zone, about half-way down the seashore but, in New England where some of the research has been done, there is an over-all migration up the shore from December to April and down again from May

* If the organ at the top of the whorl (the digestive gland) is examined microscopically, these larval stages may frequently be seen.

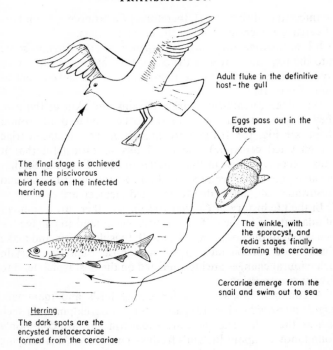

Adult fluke in the definitive host – the gull

Eggs pass out in the faeces

The final stage is achieved when the piscivorous bird feeds on the infected herring

The winkle, with the sporocyst, and redia stages finally forming the cercariae

Cercariae emerge from the snail and swim out to sea

Herring
The dark spots are the encysted metacercariae formed from the cercariae

FIG. 18. The life cycle of *Cryptocotyle lingua* (Trematoda Digenea).

to November. Infected snails are largely immobilized, usually ending up lower on the shore in May. As already stated, the active cercariae swim out of the snails and out to sea with the tide, being small, they can only swim a short distance, but are carried passively with the sea to meet the herring shoals.

The number of cercariae which emerge from one infected winkle in a single day has been estimated as 3,300, and in one year 1,300,000 have been liberated (Meyerhof & Rothschild, 1940). Upwards of 40 per cent of the winkles on a shore may be infected and there must, therefore, be astronomical numbers of cercariae liberated around the coastal waters.

It is at the time of cercarial emergence that the herrings come into the bays and coves of the coast, thereby producing a very convenient correlation between proximity of fish and concentration of cercariae.

When the cercariae penetrate the fins and skin of the fish, they encyst and cause dark marks to be produced all around them (see Fig. 18). If there are enough of these metacercariae (or encysted cercariae), the fish looks so distasteful that it causes economic loss in the fisheries of New England. Similar darkening has also been recorded on cod and other marine and freshwater fish, and is due to encysted metacercariae.

In the life history of *Cryptocotyle lingua*, there are a number of adaptations in the different stages which tend to change the behaviour of the hosts, and as a result, to isolate them and make them more conspicuous to the next host. Similarly, certain behavioural changes are also inflicted on the host which tend to favour transmission.

A common tapeworm of fish-eating birds and mammals, *Ligula intestinalis*, (Fig. 19) passes its early development in such fish as the rudd. The rudd are shoal fish and are commonly found moving about Britain's fresh waters. If a rudd is carrying the infective stage of the tapeworm (the plerocercoid), its behaviour is greatly altered. An infected rudd leaves the shoal and swims by itself, often keeled over on its side near the surface of the water. This altered behaviour has the obvious effect of making the infected fish conspicuous to the next host, and it falls an easy prey to herons, grebes, otters, etc. (T. S. C. Orr, private communication).

There are other fascinating examples of how a parasite can change the behaviour of the host so as to increase the chance of transmission, but the above examples illustrate the principles involved.

One particularly interesting case only recently discovered, is the pasture transmission of the bronchitis nematode in cattle, *Dictyocaulus viviparus*. The eggs of this parasite hatch in the

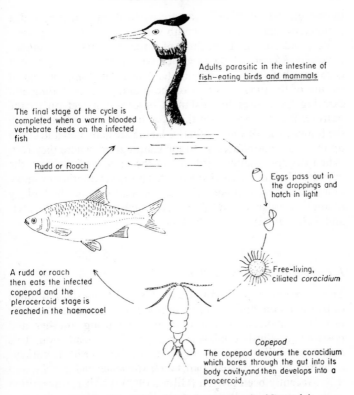

Adults parasitic in the intestine of fish—eating birds and mammals

The final stage of the cycle is completed when a warm blooded vertebrate feeds on the infected fish

Rudd or Roach

Eggs pass out in the droppings and hatch in light

A rudd or roach then eats the infected copepod and the plerocercoid stage is reached in the haemocoel

Free-living, ciliated *coracidium*

Copepod
The copepod devours the coracidium which bores through the gut into its body cavity, and then develops into a procercoid.

FIG. 19. The life cycle of *Ligula intestinalis* (Cestoda).

lungs where the adults are parasitic, and the first larval stage passes out in the dung. The first two larval stages feed on bacteria in the dung and the third larval stage or infective stage was believed to climb up the blades of grass growing around the dung, from which they were eaten by cattle, entering as a contaminant of the grass (Fig. 20). Direct field observations have, however, shown that calves (which pick up the infection) actively avoid the luxuriant grass around the dung pat and, moreover, the infective larvae are particularly sluggish, and it is unlikely that they could climb very far up blades of grass.

Very widespread on the dung of cattle and horses is a fungus, *Pilobolus Kleinii*, which needs to pass through the gut of a herbivore before it can germinate. The outstanding biological feature of the fungus, is that of the sporangium exploding and carrying the spores for distances of over ten feet on to the pasture. It has been shown that if a dung pat is 'infected' with the fungus, *Dictyocaulus* infective larvae are activated and climb up the sporangiophores on to the sporangium, where they rest. When the sporangium explodes in the middle of the day, the parasite's larvae are carried with it. This is yet another example of a parasitic transmission that depends directly on the biology of another organism, in this case, a fungus (Robinson, Poynter, and Terry, 1962).

Hyperparasitic transmission

There are only a few examples of this highly specialized mode of transmission, and one of them is still very suspect. The basic principle involved is that of a parasite using another and possibly previously established parasite, for transmission. This may best be illustrated by an example: 'blackhead' in turkeys is caused by a protozoan parasite *Histomonas meleagridis*, and it has recently been proven (Gibbs, 1962) that it is transmitted in the common poultry nematode *Heterakis gallinae*. The protozoan forms no resistant stages itself and is completely dependent on the nematode for its passage from one host to the next. It may, therefore, be controlled by controlling the nematode transmitter.

A rare protozoan parasite of man, an amoeba, *Dientamoeba fragilis*, is thought by some workers to be transmitted in the pin-worm *Enterobius vermicularis*, but this is not certain.

Hyperparasitic transmission is based on one parasite 'exploiting' the success of another, and taking advantage of the other parasite's life cycle. The origin of hyperparasitic transmission is

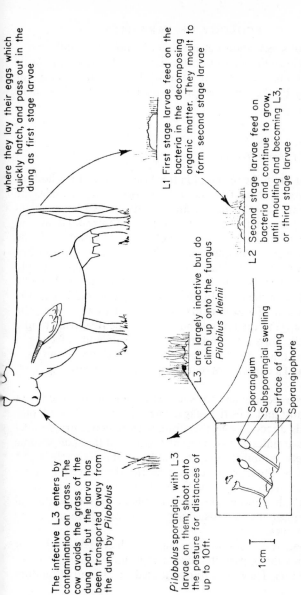

where they lay their eggs which quickly hatch, and pass out in the dung as first stage larvae

L1 First stage larvae feed on the bacteria in the decomposing organic matter. They moult to form second stage larvae

L2 Second stage larvae feed on bacteria and continue to grow, until moulting and becoming L3, or third stage larvae

L3 are largely inactive but do climb up onto the fungus *Pilobilus kleinii*

Pilobolus sporangia, with L3 larvae on them, shoot onto the pasture for distances of up to 10ft.

The infective L3 enters by contamination on grass. The cow avoids the grass of the dung pat, but the larva has been transported away from the dung by *Pilobolus*

Sporangium
Subsporangial swelling
Surface of dung
Sporangiophore

1cm

FIG. 20. The life cycle of *Dictyocaulus vivaparus* (Nematoda). One of the problems of this life cycle was finding the method by which the L3 (third larval stage) was translocated on to the pasture, thereby becoming available to the cattle in their grazing. One of the methods is to exploit the widespread fungus *Pilobolus*, which projects its sporangium for distances of up to ten feet, and carries the larvae with it.

a matter of speculation but it should be borne in mind that it may have arisen from a once free-living host adopting parasitism and taking its original parasitic fauna with it, and not necessarily by the convergence of two previously independent parasites.

Parasitoid transmission

The last group to be reviewed in this brief survey of methods of transmission is that of the parasitoid insects, for example, the ichneumons. The ichneumons are parasitic in their larval stages only, and they are frequently found in lepidopteran larvae and other insect larval stages. In some of the best-known cases, the parasitoid egg is actually injected by the female's ovipositor into the insect host. The larval parasite then grows up inside the caterpillar or insect larva, living at its expense, and finally pupates, killing the host. In this group of parasitoid insects the basic problem of transmission is simplified by restricting the parasitic stage to the juvenile phase only. The free-living motile adult itself, solves the problem of finding and infecting a suitable host, having, therefore, a high level of success in transmission, and a consequent reduction in the number of eggs laid.

The basic requirement for successful transmission is contact between host and infective stage. The general result of adaptation in this direction has, therefore, been to concentrate infective stages at times of host concentration, or at times of possible contact between infective stages and host. This principle is best illustrated by those parasites that restrict their breeding times to coincide with the breeding times of the host; and the filarial worms which concentrate their numbers in the peripheral blood to meet the blood-sucking vector, but there are many other examples.

The populations of infective stages which are responsible for the transmission of parasites must compromise between two opposing factors. They must be distributed widely and at random

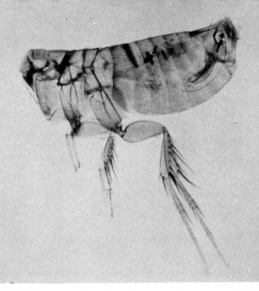

PLATE 1(a) The flea *Histrichopsylla talpae* (Insecta, Siphonaptera) ectoparasitic on the mole. Note the absence of wings and the great development of legs for jumping.

PLATE 1(b) *Cleripes biarticulata* (Insecta, Pupipara, Nycteribidae) ectoparasitic on the Horseshoe bat. Both of these groups of ectoparasites are also important as vectors in the transmission of blood Protozoa.

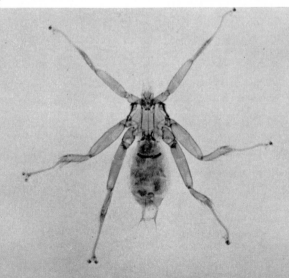

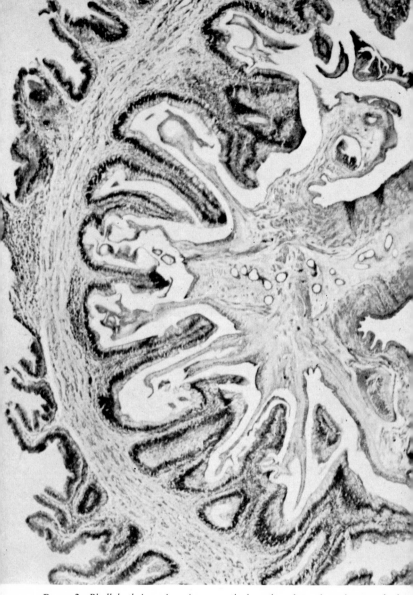

PLATE 2. *Phyllobothrium sinuosiceps*, vertical section through scolex attached to the mucosa of the spinal valve.

to ensure dispersal, while being ordered and directed enough through periodicity and other biological phenomena to ensure contact with the next host.

It is a general phenomenon that parasites with a highly efficient method of transmission produce considerably fewer potential offspring than those parasites which have a low level of successful transmission. Ichneumons which depend for their transmission on a highly modified adult insect, lay far fewer eggs than does a tapeworm or a nematode. *Ascaris*, the commonest nematode of man, lays millions of eggs and the eggs are non-motile and non-responsive. *Ascaris* transmission is largely random although the eggs show some modification, yet *Ascaris* is a highly successful helminth, its transmission being achieved by its astronomical egg output alone.

Elsewhere in the text the intimacy of the host-parasite relationship is stressed, and most authors discuss the structural, physiological, and biochemical specializations of parasites to their 'niche'. In this chapter, it has been shown that the host–parasite relationship extends beyond the period when the host and parasite are in direct contact, and into the transmitting stage. Transmission is not usually a chance or random phenomenon; instead it is often an ecologically calculated risk.

The ecological adaptations between host and parasite cannot be disregarded in the over-all ecology of parasitism. Just as adaptations are found in or on the host, so they are found in the field in order to make contact with the host.

5

Hosts and their Relationships with Parasites

HOSTS may be of various kinds and may play different roles in the lives of parasites. Because of this, a terminology has been built up to describe the different categories of host. The meanings of the names are not always obvious and a brief summary of the various types will be given. For the main part, the terminology used follows that of Baer (1952).

DEFINITIVE HOST

The definitive host is considered to be the host in which the parasite becomes adult and reaches maturity. The sheep is the definitive host of *Fasciola hepatica* and the seagull the definitive host of another fluke *Cryptocotyle lingua* (Fig. 18). In the majority of cases there is little or no doubt about the identity of the definitive host in a life cycle, but a few instances do create certain problems.

The malarial parasite, *Plasmodium vivax*, produces male and female stages while in the blood of man, but actual fertilization does not occur until the gametocytes pass into the stomach of a mosquito. Adhering closely to the definition, the mosquito is the definitive host because sexual reproduction occurs in it, but actual gametogenesis (the formation of gametocytes) takes place in man. To complicate the issue further, fertilization occurs in the blood of the blood meal while in the gut of the mosquito. Usually man is considered the definitive host and the mosquito the intermediate host, and the difficulty is overcome by this convention.

The exact definitions of types of hosts may become arbitrary, but this is not serious since they have been defined as a matter of convenience. It may be as well, however, to stress, as has been done elsewhere (see Chapter 1), that these definitions are man-made, artificial descriptions, and do not necessarily correspond to any natural order.

Another difficulty arises in those creatures which are parasitic in their larval stages, and free-living as adults, e.g. ichneumon insects, and gordian worms; both of these mature in their hosts, but reproduce when free-living. It is generally accepted that when only one host is concerned in the life history, it is the definitive host, although it is in practice referred to simply as 'the host'.

Underlying this definition of the definitive host, there has been a tendency in the past to imply that the definitive host is the most important or the essential host in the parasite's life cycle. It has also been assumed that the definitive host is of the greatest evolutionary importance in the host–parasite relationship, being the first or oldest of the hosts. Presumably, these misconceptions have arisen because the parasite passes the all-important sexual stage in it.

The modern approach, however, is to attach little fundamental significance to the term definitive host, and it is certain that the definitive host is no more essential than are the intermediate hosts, and it has not been established that the definitive host is the host of longest evolutionary standing; in some cases the reverse is likely (see Chapter 7 on the evolution of parasites).

INTERMEDIATE HOST

This category includes all the remaining hosts other than the definitive host, in which a definite developmental phase is passed. In such a familiar cycle as that of *Fasciola hepatica*, the snail *Limnaea truncatula*, is the intermediate host (Fig. 3). There may be just one intermediate host, as in the liver fluke, but in some cases, two or even three intermediate hosts may be involved in a single life cycle (Fig. 18).

The essential feature in diagnosing an intermediate host is that a definite structural or metabolic change must occur in it, and that the host is essential to the parasite. Where there is more than one intermediate host, the parasite proceeds to a further stage of development in each successive host.

In a few cases larval parasites pass a stage in a host in which *no development* occurs, but which may nevertheless be essential for successful completion of the life cycle. This type of host serves only an ecological function.

PARATENIC OR CARRIER HOST

Joyeux and Baer (1952) have described this kind of host as the '*hotes d'attente*', but say that this cannot be fully translated into English. Dismissing the alternative terms vicarious and transport host for their inadequacy they proposed the term 'paratenic host'.*

The derivation of this word is from the Greek *paratenos* = to prolong. No larval stage undergoes development in a paratenic host, and it may or may not be an essential stage in reaching the definitive host.

Among the Acanthocephala (spiny-headed worms) a paratenic host is frequently included in the life cycle, where it provides the necessary ecological link between the intermediate host and the definitive host. Larval stages of spiny-headed worms always pass through an arthropod intermediate host, and the adults are invariably found in vertebrates. Unless the arthropod intermediate host and the vertebrate definitive host come into ecological contact, the life cycle cannot be completed without the inclusion of a paratenic host.

Centrorhynchus is parasitic as an adult in a bird of prey and its larval stages are found in insects. Fully developed larval stages have also been reported from frogs, snakes, and small mammals. These small vertebrates feed largely on insects and are themselves fed on by birds of prey. They therefore provide the necessary ecological link between arthropods and predatory birds.

* Cameron (1956) adopts the alternative name 'carrier host' to describe this category of host.

The small vertebrates are, in this case, paratenic hosts, and it is through them that the parasite is passively carried from the arthropod intermediate host to the vertebrate definitive host.

VECTORS

The term vector has an indefinite significance and has been used to describe almost all kinds of host, except definitive hosts. One category, however, remains that is not adequately covered by the preceding definitions, that is the role of mechanical transmitter.

In a few parasites, notably blood protozoa, the parasite is transmitted from definitive host to definitive host by a blood-sucking vector. No development occurs in the vector, and the vector, although essential, does nothing more than a hypodermic needle could do.

A number of important protozoa in the Tropics, e.g. *Trypanosoma evansi*, which is transmitted mechanically by Tabanid flies, depend on vectors. *Trypanosoma evansi* causes 'Surra' in domesticated animals, especially camels, horses, and cattle (see Fig. 28).

Mechanical transmitters or vectors are therefore of considerable worldwide economic importance. On a smaller scale, and much nearer home, is the blood parasitic protozoan of frogs, *Lankesterella*. The entire development of the parasite occurs in the cells lining the blood vessels (the endothelial cells); the sporozoites or infective stages are released into the blood and enter the blood cells and may be taken up in the blood meal of a leech. The leech can then infect another frog while sucking its blood, or it may infect another frog on being eaten by it.

In some ways a vector is similar to a paratenic host, but the paratenic host is always found in *addition* to other intermediate hosts, while the vector is not. A paratenic host is not necessarily essential in the life of the parasite, whereas a vector is absolutely essential.

RESERVOIR HOSTS

Reservoir hosts do not form a strictly delimited biological category, but as the term is in common use, a few brief examples will be given.

The chief use of the phrase is in the aetiology of diseases; in this context it is familiar in medical and veterinary work, and it usually describes a definitive host which acts as an outside source or reservoir of infection.

One of the best known examples is another blood parasitic protozoan in tropical Africa, *Trypanosoma brucei*. This parasite infects cattle and causes 'nagana', the symptoms of which include intermittent fever, emaciation and anaemia, sometimes resulting in death. *T. brucei* is transmitted by an intermediate host, the tsetse fly (*Glossina palpalis*).

The tsetse fly sucks the blood of domesticated and wild ungulates alike, and consequently carries the parasite to all the wild game in parts of tropical Africa. Nagana is found only in domesticated cattle and the wild animals are naturally resistant to the disease. In this example, all the carriers provide a continual source of infection and are termed reservoir hosts.

Trypanosoma gambiense is the closely related parasite of man which causes sleeping sickness in Africa. The sleeping symptom is caused by the later stages of the parasite entering the cerebro-spinal fluid of the spinal cord. The intermediate hosts are species of tsetse fly, and many animals such as pigs, dogs, goats, and antelopes, in addition to man have a high rate of infection. Man's domesticated animals act as a source of infection for *Trypanosoma gambiense*, just as he himself acts as a source of their infection.

Parasites as indicators of host relationships

In the animal kingdom there are found certain ancient groups which have survived unchanged over great epochs of geological time. They are popularly named 'living fossils' or 'relics', and

TABLE 1. Illustration of the relationship between Hosts and Parasites

Type of Host	Stage of parasite in the host	Necessity of the host to the parasite	Role of the host in the life cycle
1. Definitive	Adult	Essential	Development and maturation
2. Intermediate	Juvenile	Essential	Development and transmission
3. Paratenic	Juvenile	May be an ecological necessity	Ecological link only
4. Vector*	Juvenile	Essential	Transmission only

are obviously important to students of animal taxonomy and evolution.

Living fossils have persisted because they possess some outstanding physiological adaptation, or because they have remained unspecialized or because of some geographical or ecological isolation. Isolation has spared them the rigours of competition and therefore made possible their survival. The parasites of these archaic groups are of considerable theoretical interest to parasitologists.

Some typical living fossils are: lampreys (jawless ectoparasites of fish), coelacanths, sturgeons, lungfish, tortoises and turtles, and monotremes (or egg-laying mammals, the echidna or spiny anteater and the duck-billed platypus of Australasia).

The parasites of many of these primitive vertebrates are unknown but some of the tapeworms have received a little attention (reviewed by Wardle and McLeod, 1952). Two very ancient fish, *Amia* and *Polypterus*, known to zoologists today

* Also used extensively as an epidemiological term.

as living forms and to palaentologists as fossils, both carry aberrant tapeworms peculiar to each species. *Amia* carries *Haplobothrium** in its intestine, and *Polypterus* carries *Ancistrocephalus*.

Another family of tapeworms parasitic in birds is the Davaineidae, which is believed to be of great antiquity. The Davaineidae parasitize flightless birds (ratites) including ostriches, galliform birds, and the tinamous of South America.

An ancient subfamily of tapeworms, the Linstowinae, are typically parasitic in egg-laying mammals (monotremes), pouched mammals (marsupials), edentates (sloths and armadillos), lemurs, and insectivores. These are all very primitive groups of mammals.

Primitive parasites are often considered primitive because they are found in primitive hosts, similarly hosts may be thought primitive because of the nature of their parasitic burden. It is clear that care must be taken to evaluate the true significance of these facts and not to draw from them conclusions that may well be invalid. Where possible, speculations about animal relationships should be related to fossil or other geological evidence, and the highly intriguing parasitological evidence, as with other evidence from living species, should be used to support rather than derive any argument.

Individual species of ancient hosts carry their own peculiar parasites, a phenomenon which can be taken a stage further, to cover groups of hosts. *Amia*, described above, is characteristically parasitized by *Haplobothrium*, an individual host carrying a specific tapeworm. The Davaineidae and the Linstowiinae are whole families of related parasites which are typically found in whole groups of primitive hosts. Parasites may be useful as biological indicators of host relationships at species, family, and even order level.

In some cases whole divisions of the animal kingdom are characterized by unique groups of parasites. Elasmobranchs, the group of fish which include sharks, skates, rays, and rabbit

---

* *Haplobothrium* is so unusual that zoologists have classified it in a separate family on its own, the Haplobothriidae.

fish, are believed by zoologists to form a distinct and related group; they are believed to have originated from a single ancestor (see Fig. 21). The parasitological evidence in support of this is also most neatly supplied by tapeworms. There are two orders of tapeworms (the Tetraphyllida and Tetrarhynchida) which are unique as adults in elasmobranch fishes.

Parasites can be used as zoological evidence to indicate the evolutionary age and relationships of their hosts, but only if this is done with care and common sense. Cameron (1956) goes to great lengths to trace the general evolution of vertebrates from a study of their parasites; this is often interesting but can only be of use to confirm or support fossil evidence or geological facts.

There are so many ecological and physiological factors interacting during the evolution of host groups that the present-day status of the parasites need not necessarily be related exactly to their original status. As a result of host specificity, a certain proportion of the original parasites are likely to have remained in the original host species or its progeny.

6

Host Specificity

ONE of the fundamental concepts of parasitology is host specificity, and a study of it is not only interesting in itself but is essential to a full understanding of parasitism. Host specificity is the name given to the frequently encountered phenomenon of parasites being confined to certain hosts.

Many phytophagous insects, both as adults, e.g. bugs, and as larvae, e.g. caterpillars, feed only on certain plants. The giant panda feeds almost exclusively on bamboo shoots, and the koala bear depends on the leaves of certain eucalyptus trees for its diet. Highly modified flowers are often specifically dependent on particular insects for their pollination; similarly, different species of dung beetle are found only in the dung of certain animals. In these cases, the flowers may be considered 'specific' to the pollinating insects and the dung beetles are 'specific' to the dung of a single creature.

Specificity of various kinds is widely distributed throughout the plant and animal kingdoms, and must not be thought of as being confined to parasites. 'Host specificity' is the name given to the form of specificity found among parasites.

It will, no doubt, be apparent that the parasites of a jellyfish or an earthworm are not infective to man. A parasite, structurally, physiologically and biochemically adapted to its jellyfish host, is too specialized in one direction successfully to enter a host like man; it is this simple idea and the mechanisms which control it, that is the basis of host specificity. Successfully to parasitize a single host, a parasite must be so highly specialized in one direction that it is thereby prevented from increasing its host range. Host specificity is based on the parasite's adaptations to the structure and physiology of its single microhabitat, and a fully adapted parasite reaches a level of intimacy that leads to a dependence.

Parasitologists have speculated extensively on the origin and mechanisms of host specificity, and the modern approach is to emphasize the dynamic nature of the relationship between parasite and host.

Authorities agree that host specificity has resulted from two lines of development in the evolution of the host–parasite relationship; parallel evolution of host and parasite, and ecology.

As a starting point, consider an hypothetical ancestral host having its own primitive parasitic burden, peculiar to it and modified to parasitize only the single ancestral host. The ancient host then evolved and, through gradual changes of structure and physiology, gave rise to a number of similar but distinct host forms (Fig. 21).

Concurrent with the evolution of the hosts, would need to be the evolution of the parasites, and selection would ensure that the parasites 'kept pace' with the changes in their hosts. Each of these new hosts would, therefore, have its own peculiar parasitic burden, similar to, but distinct from, the parasites of the ancestral host.

It is believed that such evolutionary changes were very gradual, and it is reasonable to suppose that the slight changes in the host were paralleled by corresponding adaptations in their parasites. If such a mechanism did occur, and it is generally accepted that it did, it would not be limited to closely related hosts, but could occur over the whole spectrum of potential hosts.

If parasites do evolve with their hosts as has been suggested, it would be expected that hosts of great antiquity (p. 63) would harbour a zoologically primitive parasite burden. Furthermore, a group parasitizing a wide range of related hosts, can be considered as having evolved with them and, therefore, to be of considerable antiquity.

All this so far is calculated speculation, but it will be clear that if host specificity did develop along the lines described

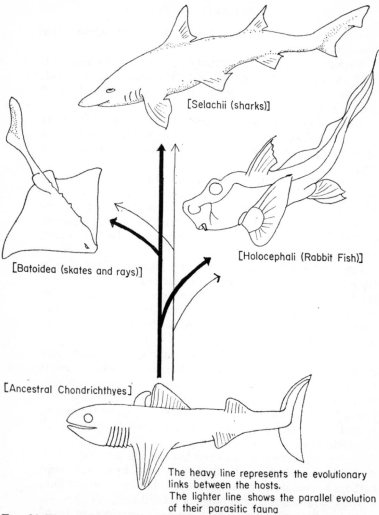

[Selachii (sharks)]

[Batoidea (skates and rays)]

[Holocephali (Rabbit Fish)]

[Ancestral Chondrichthyes]

The heavy line represents the evolutionary
links between the hosts.
The lighter line shows the parallel evolution
of their parasitic fauna

FIG. 21. The relationship between the evolution of hosts and their parasites.
The known zoological affinities between hosts are sometimes closely reflected
by the systematic relations of their parasites, giving evidence of the parasites'
age and also on the development of host specificity.

above, a certain amount of circumstantial evidence should be available.

Perhaps the strongest evidence is that closely-related parasites are often found on closely-related hosts. For example, there is a group of ectoparasitic insects, the Pupipara, the members of a major family of which, the Nycteribiidae, are found only on bats. Related hosts of monophyletic origin (all having evolved from a single host) are often parasitized by a whole order or class of parasites exclusive to themselves (see Fig. 21). As illustrations of this, the tapeworm family Taeniidae may be taken, the members of which, as adults, parasitize mammalian hosts only. Similarly skates, rays, and sharks which are grouped together as the Elasmobrancha (implying that they are phylogenetically related), are the exclusive hosts of the tapeworm orders Tetraphyllida and Tetrarhyncha (Fig. 21).

To correlate the facts with the evolutionary postulate above, it may be assumed, for example, that the ancestral elasmobranch carried in its intestine an ancestral tapeworm. Through the course of evolution, first the fish evolved and with it the parasite, each new fish harbouring its own peculiar tapeworm. The present-day result is that elasmobranch fish harbour two orders of tapeworm peculiar to themselves, due to the parallel development of host and parasite; all of the hosts carry their own tapeworms and all the tapeworms are related.

There are a number of discrepancies in the general rule of parallel evolution leading to specificity, discrepancies which may be explained largely on ecological grounds. If the original ancestral elasmobranch previously discussed became infected through feeding on crabs, the parasite would depend for its continued existence on this ecological link. Let us imagine that one of the evolutionary branches from this fish no longer fed on crabs, then the parasite would disappear from this branch, because of the omission of the essential ecological link. Such ecological evidence may be postulated as an explanation of the many apparent anomalies in host specificity.

Similarly, phylogenetically unrelated hosts may be sufficiently related ecologically to share the same parasites. Man shares some of his ectoparasites with bats, and it is believed that this is a result of their both having lived together in caves in pre-historic times. Young children often fall victim to the parasites of pet dogs and cats with which they are in continual contact. Close relatives of the ectoparasites on rabbits are found on shearwaters, in this case it is thought that the ecological link is due to the adoption of rabbit burrows by the birds.

Superimposed on the basic phylogenetic specificity is an overall ecological specificity. As the hosts and their parasites were evolving, parasites radiated out to infect ecologically related hosts. Sprent has summed up this distinction between the origin of members in a parasitic fauna by calling those which evolved with the hosts the 'heirlooms', while those picked up more recently, through ecological contact, the 'souvenirs'.

In the study of parasitic disease, it is often necessary to infect a laboratory animal to facilitate the maintenance of a labora-tory infection. To do this, mice, rats, cats, etc., are used as experimental hosts, and they are frequently found to be very suitable for this purpose. In nature, however, they are not naturally included in the host range because of some in-sufficient ecological link.

On a wider plane, the geography of suitable hosts may also affect parasitic incidence. Potential hosts may be found on separate continents, so that the possible contact between host and parasite is prevented, parasites therefore not reaching otherwise susceptible hosts.

The dynamic state of host specificity may be considered to be the product of the complex of evolution and ecology, which is itself in a state of flux.

It has been shown that host specificity is a result of extensive specialization of a parasite to one host, with the consequent loss of adaptability to others. Often a single morphological or physiological feature of the host is particularly demanding and has led to a consequent adaptation of its parasites. Because of this, it is quite usual to find that the host range is limited by a single profound structural or physiological adaptation of the parasite.

An example of such a structural 'limiting factor', found by Knorre (1937), is in the leech *Helobdella solae*. The posterior sucker is adapted in shape and size to the ctenoid scales of the flat fishes of the genus *Solea*, and is therefore unable to attach to other fish.

The structural basis of host specificity may also be demonstrated by the monogenetic flukes parasitic on the gills of fish. Llewellyn (1956 and 1960) has shown that the clamps of the genera *Diclidophora*, *Discocotyle* and *Plectanocotyle*, are all closely modified to hold on to the gill filaments of their fish hosts. In both these cases, the leech and the monogeneans, extensive morphological specialization to the host has greatly restricted the parasites' host range. The intricate structure of many tapeworms has also been shown to be closely correlated with the villus structure of the host (Williams).

There has been as yet insufficient research to elucidate the exact physiological basis of host specificity, and in this field, the evidence is more circumstantial. Rogers (1962) has suggested that for many infective stages of nematodes to hatch and develop further inside their hosts, they require an essential biochemical or biophysical factor. It is suggested that the parasite can no longer synthesize a necessary compound and that it depends on its host for this. Naturally, the parasite will be specific only to those hosts which are able to provide such a compound. Such an explanation would go a long way towards explaining the physiological basis of host specificity. Perhaps the best evidence for this is found when scientists attempt to culture parasites outside their hosts. They have demanded a large number of highly complicated chemicals to complete their life cycles successfully.

Further circumstantial evidence is provided by the relative specificity of the parasites of different host tissues. It is found that parasites of the blood and lymph, for example, tend to be more specific than parasites of the gut lumen. Similarly, blood-feeding parasites of the gut wall are more specific than are lumen-dwelling parasites of the gut. Sweeping generalizations of this sort do, however, include many exceptions.

The blood provides a constant and complex niche in the body of a host, while the lumen of the gut is more variable, being liable to fluctuation of contents and physical conditions. The ecological demands of the blood are complex and exacting and to be a successful blood parasite demands extensive and therefore inflexible adaptation. To be a successful parasite of the gut lumen, where overall adaptations are necessary, but a degree of tolerance to variation is also required, is to be adapted in a slightly different direction. This tolerance enables gut dwelling parasites to have a wider host range.

A variable degree of host specificity may also be found in the different stages of a single parasite. Digenetic flukes tend to be far more specific in their larval stages. In the snail, which is the first intermediate host of all digenetic flukes, are produced the sporocyst, redial and cercarial stages of development. In the case of the well-known liver fluke *Fasciola hepatica*, *Limnaea truncatula* is the only species of snail in Britain which can be used as an intermediate host, although it must be added that other snails have been found infected in other parts of the world. A very striking contrast appears, however, between the restricted host range of the larvae and the wide host range of the adult. In its adult stage *F. hepatica* has been recorded from the liver bile ducts of rabbits, goats, oxen, horses, pigs, asses, cats, killer whales, and man, in addition to its more familiar definitive host, the sheep (Dawes, 1956).

Cryptocotyle lingua (Fig. 18), for example, uses only the edible winkle, *Littorina littorea*, as its first intermediate host, showing a high level of host specificity at this stage in its life cycle. In the winkle it undergoes considerable structural and metabolic changes. Following this, the second intermediate host is a fish, where the metacercarial stage lies dormant in the skin and fins. A number of different fish are used as second intermediate hosts, and this is correlated with the almost complete absence of metabolic development. Similarly, the adult fluke is found in a number of gulls and terns.

These examples illustrate a correlation between the extent of development in a host and the degree of host specificity. Development imposes certain metabolic demands and these the host must be able to supply. The physiological requirements of gross morphological or metabolic development tend to limit the range to only one or to a few suitable hosts, which are able to meet the parasites' needs. In the cases where the host is merely an ecological link, and the parasite therefore passes through no developmental stage, there can be wider host range.

The degree of host specificity may relate therefore to the particular tissue parasitized (as in the case of blood) or it may vary with the developmental stages in a parasite's life cycle, as was shown in flukes. It has been suggested that, in both cases, the host range of the parasite is lowered owing to the increased physiological demands and subsequent specialization.

Some parasites show a different sort of specialization. The natural consequence of the kinds of specificity so far discussed, is for each host to carry its own peculiar parasitic burden; however, a few parasites are able to parasitize a wide range of hosts. The host range of the well-known trichina worm, *Trichinella spiralis*, for example, seems to be limited only on ecological grounds, surviving in every experimental host tried. Although this is the exception, there are some parasites that have become adapted in a different way, showing a wide host specificity.

There is ample evidence to show how host specificity came about, parasites having become self-limiting through extensive specialization to one host. The phenomenon of host specificity itself supports the hypothesis about the origin and evolution of parasites, for host specificity is not only a feature of parasitism, it is a natural consequence of it.

7

The Evolution of Parasitism

THE origin of parasitism, like most origins, is largely a subject for speculation, as there exists very little factual evidence, and any postulates must be based on circumstantial arguments alone. This is no reason for avoiding consideration of the evolution of the parasitic way of life, but it is from this rather shaky premise that we must begin.

The course of evolution cannot usually be tested experimentally, but it is useful to remember that the product of evolution (the animals living today), can be studied in some detail. If we draw an analogy between evolution and an experiment, this inverted approach, unlike many others in science, attempts to establish the conditions of the experiment from the observable results, and the course of the reaction from its product. It is the course of evolution that we are attempting to infer from a study of existing forms.

It would be misleading to think that the animals alive today demonstrate the road along which the most advanced members have travelled. A comparative study of living forms may, however, illustrate some of the intermediaries between the free-living and the parasitic habit, and therefore throw light on possible lines of specialization that have led to parasitism.

Parasites are believed to have existed for a very considerable time, although there is no fossil evidence for this. The extensive modifications demanded from the niche must have taken many millions of years to come about, as must the parallel complexities of the host reaction.

Parasites do not belong to a single taxomonic group and it is clear that parasitism has been adopted independently by many widely separated groups, each following a slightly different line of specialization.

In addition to including a wide range of structure and biology, parasites today, all being at different stages of development, may be used to form the outline of the evolutionary paths taken.

The evolution of parasites is likely to have been controlled by a few fundamental factors, and it is these common denominators of evolution that are the chief concern of this chapter. There are two useful starting points: one is the comparison of existing parasites with their free-living relatives and the postulation of links between them; or more usually, the comparison of the free-living stages of parasites with those of free-living organisms. Another approach is to consider possible exploitation of existing associations which may have developed into parasitism, from a previous and less dependent association.

In all cases the most important line of study is to investigate the preadaptations which would prepare a free-living creature for a parasitic way of life.

'Preadaptation', as the word suggests, refers to the previous adaptation necessary for an organism to change to another way of life. Preadaptation as a feature of evolution is not always given the weight it deserves, for it has been instrumental in the evolution of many groups, not only of parasites. Much of the biology of marine isopods, for example, also lent itself to use on land. It is believed that this was a preadaptation of isopods to a terrestrial existence and was important in their successful conquest of the land.

The development of protective plates by the typical woodlouse (an isopod) was a preadaptation to the terrestrial way of life as were the methods of breeding and the oviparity.

Much of the speculation about the evolution of parasitism is zoologically acceptable, but the most fundamental difficulty is the very nature of the change from the free-living to the parasitic existence. The modern view on evolution is that the evolutionary process is based on gradual changes which persist over millions of years and gradually become incorporated into the biology of their possessors. If this view is correct, and changes are slow, extending over many generations, it is zoologically unacceptable that a fully adapted free-living organism could become sufficiently modified to make a success of parasitism in one great and hazardous leap! The parasitic niche demands such a high degree of specialization that it is impossible to imagine a wholly unadapted organism making even a partial success without some previous experience.

Armed with the benefits of preadaptation this step becomes more plausible. Each preadaptation minimizing the extent of the step and reducing the demands of the new way of life. Every preadaptive feature of the potential parasite's biology, that is features shared between the existing habitat and 'proposed' parasitic one, makes more possible the adoption of parasitism. It is therefore of particular interest to trace the evolution of parasitism through the exploitation of preadaptations.

To illustrate the importance of preadaptation in the evolution of parasitism, the course of development taken by *Trypanosoma*, the causative organism of 'sleeping sickness' in man will be followed. *Trypanosoma* is a Protozoan flagellate, and is a widespread genus, the various species being parasitic in the circulatory systems of vertebrates (see Fig. 22).

It is believed that *Trypanosoma* evolved from a *Phytomonas*-like ancestor a closely related genus of flagellates. *Phytomonas* swims about in the latex of euphorbiacean plants, and it is from this ecologically distant organism that the blood-living *Trypanosoma* evolved. It would seem at first sight almost impossible for the plant parasite to develop into a blood parasite of vertebrates but, through preadaptation, the change is quite plausible.

Phytomonas is transmitted from one plant to another when accidentally taken up by plant feeding bugs. Bugs feed with mouth-parts adapted to pierce the plant cuticle and suck up the nutritive plant juices; it is in these juices that *Phytomonas* lives, depending on the insect vector for its transport to new plants.

It is believed that the original stage in the plant became increasingly adapted to its insect intermediate host, until it was more a parasite of the insect than of the plant, the plant parasi-

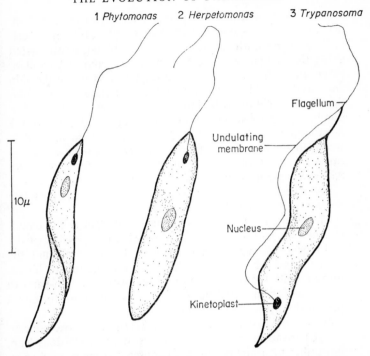

1 *Phytomonas*   2 *Herpetomonas*   3 *Trypanosoma*

Flagellum

Undulating membrane

Nucleus

10μ

Kinetoplast

Parasitic in the latex of euphorbiacean plants

Parasitic in the gut of flies and other insects

Parasitic in the blood of vertebrates and transmitted by blood sucking insects

FIG. 22. Three closely related protozoan flagellates of the family Trypanosomatidae. These, although widely separated in their biology and site of parasitization, may be stages in an evolutionary path from plant latex to vertebrate blood.

tic stage gradually being reduced. In this stage the adoption of insect parasitism would have been relatively simple owing to the previous adaptation to the insect vector. Such a hypothesis is further supported by the occurrence of *Herpetomonas*, a related flagellate commonly found in insects today.

The next stage in this evolutionary recapitulation is to link the parasite in the gut of a phytophagous (plant feeding) insect, to *Trypanosoma*, a parasite of vertebrate blood. It was stated above that the bug was adapted for piercing and sucking plant tissue, the same mouth-parts preadapted it to pierce the skin and drink the blood of vertebrates. Correlating this evolutionary speculation with biological fact, there occur a few families of blood-sucking bugs (including the bed bugs), the most important being the Reduviidae. *Triatoma megista*, a Reduviid bug, is the chief carrier of *Trypanosoma cruzi*, the causative agent of Chagas' disease, a fatal form of South American trypanosomiasis (see Fig. 22).

It is, therefore, with some confidence that we can postulate the adoption of blood feeding by the bug.

Meanwhile the flagellates remained in the gut of the blood-feeding bug, and in this way gradually became physiologically and biochemically adapted to living in the blood medium, the food of its host. This physiological preadaptation to blood, together with the preadaptation of the insects' mouth-parts to blood feeding, prepared the *Trypanosoma* progenitor for blood parasitism of the vertebrate host.

It may now be appreciated that *Trypanosoma* was able to adopt parasitism, not through one great and hazardous leap, but rather by a number of small consecutive steps, made possible by preadaptation and ecological suitability.

This is a simplified account but it is believed that the details may be true in outline. The actual evolution of the genus *Trypanosoma* can be traced even farther; some species being transmitted by other insects, e.g. fleas, that have been secondarily incorporated into the life cycle. In this case, it is thought that the flea has accidentally ingested some of the parasites while taking a blood meal, and a further life cycle has been established. Prior to its blood meal, the flea injects an anti-coagulant salivary secretion into the wound, and it is at this stage that the blood parasite is inoculated into the vertebrate bloodstream.

The above example of preadaptation and ecological evolution illustrates how the apparently impossible step from the latex of a plant to the blood of a vertebrate is made possible, if each stage is preceded by a morphological or physiological pre-adaptation prior to its adoption. The phytophagous bug had mouth-parts which were equally well adapted to both plant and blood feeding.

Another example of an evolutionary path made possible through preadaptation is found in nematodes. In addition to nematodes which are parasitic on plants and animals, some are found free living in the sea, freshwater and soil. It is from these free-living relatives that existing parasites are thought to have evolved, and any ecological links may be of evolutionary importance.

Some of the free-living nematodes live in dung, just as certain dung beetles do, and they are often peculiar to the dung of one host. In this microhabitat the worms live on bacteria and must be able to tolerate an anaerobic medium, a greatly fluctuating osmotic pressure and a range of biophysical and biochemical complexes all characteristic of this habitat.

If such a dung-dwelling nematode were to ascend a blade of grass and were to be accidentally eaten by the animal that had provided its home for so long, the worm would have the chance of adopting the parasitic way of life.

Such a worm would be largely preadapted to survive in the colon of its host. The contents of the colon and rectum are chiefly excreta with dense populations of bacteria; the nema-tode would, therefore, be preadapted to this medium, its bacterial food, and the microenvironmental conditions that it would encounter.

Relating this hypothetical idea to fact, nematodes are found free-living in dung, there is evidence to suggest that some of the more primitive parasitic forms are to be found in the posterior parts of the intestine, and the free-living stages of such parasites live in dung and feed on bacteria. This is of course an over-simplified explanation as it by-passes the big hurdle of over-coming the enzymic secretions, etc., of the host; nevertheless it exemplifies a possible preadaptive route.

Again it may be seen that the ecological barrier separating the free-living nematode in dung and the parasitic nematode in the gut may be very small as a result of preadaptation.

One final example of preadaptation, this time a parasite of insects, will be discussed. Among the free-living nematodes are some which feed on fungus in the soil. To feed successfully on fungus, an animal must be able to digest the peculiar chemical compound of the hyphal wall, which is composed of fungal cellulose. Chemically, fungal cellulose contains chitin, a nitrogenous polysaccharide, the same compound that is the chief constituent of insects' cuticle. A fungus-feeding animal is therefore potentially an insect parasite, and it is not surprising that some nematodes have adopted insect parasitism.

Preadaptation, whether morphological, physiological, or ecological, supplies the preparation for the devastating change from the free-living to the parasitic mode of life. The greater the degree of preadaptation, the less demanding is the change. Preadaptiveness is, however, a purely potential quality and is dependent on the environment for providing a suitable opportunity to exploit it.

The phylum Platyhelminthes includes, in addition to the parasitic classes Trematoda (flukes) and Cestoda (tapeworms), the free-living class Turbellaria. Among the Turbellaria are the familiar freshwater flatworms *Planaria*, *Polycelis* and *Dendrocoelium*, commonly found during the day under stones in ponds and streams.

Many turbellarians have tended to form associations and they include a large number of independently developed examples of commensals and symbionts. A related group of flatworms, the Temnocephala, are always found attached to the outsides of freshwater Crustacea and other invertebrate groups. The exact relationship is not clear but the flatworms appear to do no harm and are carried passively about attached to the legs or carapace of the crustacean, apparently using the crustacean for dispersion.

Convoluta is a marine flatworm which inhabits sand and mud around the coast of Brittany and the Channel Islands. It has no functional gut and in its place carries symbiotic algae, depending on them for the synthesis of its organic food.

There is even one turbellarian flatworm *Fecampia*, that is a true parasite in its adult stages. The fully developed free-living larva penetrates the body cavity of a marine isopod crustacean (which looks like a woodlouse) called *Idotea neglecta*, and matures in it, becoming an adult. Many other cases are known of animal associations between turbellarians and other creatures, particularly among the order Rhabdocoelida, the order from which the flukes and tapeworms are believed to have originated.

In the past the possibility of symbiosis or commensalism leading to parasitism has been discredited on a little fossil evidence and because of the unlikelihood of altering a previously intimate relationship (Baer). It is possible however that one member of such a previous association evolved at a faster rate than the other, or not in parallel with it, the over-all result being a change in the type of bond between the animals. The possibility of differential evolution in an existing animal association leading to parasitism, although highly speculative, is all the same plausible.

The basic organization of the free-living turbellarian bears close resemblance to that of the parasitic flatworms and the fact that they are related is undisputed. Because the parasitic flatworms are descended from the Turbellaria, and they in turn show a tendency to form animal associations, it is possible that some parasites may have developed from a less intimate or different kind of animal association.

Parasitism has come about in many animals and has followed diverse routes but there exists one common denominator in all these evolutionary paths—that of preadaptation.

8

The Influence of Parasites on their Hosts

ONE of the most familiar examples of a natural equilibrium is the numerical correspondence between the mortality rate of young and the number of young produced. The number of eggs laid by the cod may be in the millions, whereas with the dogfish it is in the tens; however, the number of adult cod and dogfish remains fairly constant. In species with a high juvenile mortality, a proportionately large number of eggs is laid – as is the case with many parasites. The successful parasite has reached a balance between the external environment and the number of eggs laid.

At the more intimate level of host–parasite relationship, when host and parasite are in contact, a comparable equilibrium has been reached.

Vertebrate host defence mechanisms

The host reaction to parasitic infection is twofold; firstly, the basic immunological reaction to the presence of a foreign body and, secondly, the other tissue reactions.

Immunity responses are aimed at destroying a foreign body or inactivating a particular foreign compound and thereafter being resistant to further infection by it. Tissue reactions are aimed more at isolating the parasite by forming a cyst or walling it off from the host's tissues. Such tissue reactions are parasite-induced and are the direct result of the parasites' secretions, excretory products, movements, etc., on the host's cells.

Both tissue and immunological reactions function at biochemical or cellular level, and natural acquired immunity is virtually restricted to those parasites that come into contact with the bloodstream. All host defence mechanisms are used to combat parasitic infection.

TISSUE REACTIONS

(i) *Inflammation*. Inflammation, as a result of parasitic infestation, frequently occurs in response to tissue-dwelling parasites, but it would be misleading to imagine that the defences are aimed exclusively at parasites. Host defences are basically biochemical responses to alien chemicals, although these alien chemicals may be of parasitic origin, they need not necessarily be so. All host reactions are general responses to chemical invasion, which may be used against parasites. Inflammation is a direct response to the presence of a parasite, and is provoked by the death or destruction of host cells. The first host response to tissue damage appears to be histamine secretion, which is immediately followed by capillary dilation. Capillary dilation causes an increased amount of blood to be brought to the damaged site and brings with it phagocytes, leucocytes, and lymphocytes, important white corpuscles of the blood. Eosinophilia, or an increased number of eosinophilic leucocytes is often characteristic of helminth infections.

Inflammation follows a uniform cyclic build-up, often resulting in the formation of an exudate, partly derived from the blood, partly from the tissues, and consisting of blood plasma, leucocytes and macrophages. Inflammation is often accompanied by heat production (possibly due to interference with the nerves which control heat dissipation), and may be considered as the microscopic response of the host to the presence of an alien chemical or to local mechanical destruction.

The later stages of the inflammatory response may include scab formation by fibrosis and, if prolonged, may result in calcareous cyst formation. Cyst formation tends to encapsulate the offending parasitic organism. Such capsules are found, for example, in the muscle stages of *Trichinella spiralis*, and sometimes *Schistosoma* eggs also become encapsulated by the host.

Hyperactivity of the lymphatic system, caused by infestation, is a part of inflammation and is associated in man with the well-known throbbing in the primary lymph nodes.

ABNORMAL GROWTH

One of the possible consequences of parasitic infestation is a change in the growth pattern of a parasitized tissue. The change may be one of four main types, all resulting in an abnormal form of growth.

(*i*) *Hyperplasia.* Hyperplasia is caused by an increased activity in cell metabolism, resulting in an accelerated rate of cell division. This leads to a greater total number of cells, but not necessarily an increase in their absolute size. Hyperplasia often succeeds inflammation, being due to an excess level of tissue repair, more cells being produced than are actually required. 'Pipe stem liver' in animals infected with *Fasciola hepatica*, is a result of hyperplasia. In this case the bile duct epithelium grows extensively, becoming corrugated and later thickened by calcareous deposition.

(*ii*) *Hypertrophy.* Hypertrophy is an increase in the size of the host cells and is typically the result of some intracellular blood parasites. The common malarial parasite, *Plasmodium vivax*, passes a stage in red blood cells and during this period causes them to enlarge. Many parasitic infections evoke hyperactivity (over-activity) of the spleen; the spleen is a centre of antibody production and hyperactivity causes an enlargement of the spleen, a disorder known as splenomegaly. African children, frequently seen in photographs with 'pot bellies', are suffering from splenomegaly. (However this may also be a symptom of malnutrition.)

(*iii*) *Metaplasia.* Metaplasia is caused by a tissue changing its basic structure and becoming another type of tissue, without the intervention of embryonic tissue. *Paragonimus westermanii*, a fluke parasitic in the lungs of carnivores including man, evokes a metaplasial response in the host tissue, and becomes surrounded by a layer of epithelial cells.

(*iv*) *Neoplasia*. Neoplasia is a growth of a new structure, a tumour, from an existing tissue. Extensive research is being carried out at present into the structure and metabolism of tumours, the basis of cancer, and exact definition is essentially speculative. Neoplasms may be benign or malignant, and may take the form among others, of a carcinoma (a cancer of the epithelial tissue), or of a sarcoma (a cancer of the connective tissue). Smyth (1962) lists ten parasites which are believed to be associated with tumours in mammals. They include examples from the Protozoa, the Trematoda (flukes), the Cestoda (tapeworms), and the Nematoda (roundworms).

It is firmly established that three helminths definitely cause cancer: *Cysticerus fasciolaris*, which is the larval stage of the tapeworm *Taenia taeniaformis*, and is found in the liver of rats; and the adult stage of the nematode *Spirocerca lupi*, which evokes sarcoma formation in the oesophageal tissues of dogs; *Schistosoma haematobium*, the human blood fluke, is also known to cause carcinoma of the bladder.

In a time of concentrated cancer research, it is interesting to note that a wide spectrum of parasites can cause tumours. The biochemical basis of tumour formation has not yet been elucidated, although a great deal of research has been carried out with *Cysticercus fasciolaris*, and much has been learnt. There is some evidence to support the theory that cancer caused by tapeworms is related to the calcareous bodies usually found in the cysticerci (Dunning & Curtis 1946).

There are a number of ways in which host tissues may respond to parasitic infestation: as we have seen, the primary reaction is that of inflammation, a response to the presence of a foreign substance. More fundamental changes in tissue size and structure may result from parasitic invasion. When directed at the parasite, all these reactions may be considered as the host defence against invasion. They tend to destroy the parasite or to limit its numbers, and thereby reach a level of mutual tolerance. It may be emphasized that these are parasite-provoked host reactions, and that the well-adapted parasite must be able to withstand the host reaction, just as the well-adapted host must tolerate a parasitic invasion.

The effect of the parasite on the invertebrate host

Until more investigation has been carried out, it will not be certain which effects of parasitism are the host reaction and which are the direct effects of the parasite on the host. The distinction may be an arbitrary one, because the host reaction is itself a response evoked by the parasite. Bearing in mind this slight distinction, some of the effects of parasites on invertebrate hosts will be discussed. As before, the extent of our knowledge of the actual effects is small and what is known chiefly concerns arthropods and most of that is about insects and crustaceans.

The most intimate and probably the most important realm of host–parasite relationship is at the invisible level of biochemistry and, although some parasites have been shown to have very dramatic structural effects on their hosts, interesting as these are, they are of little fundamental importance.

(*i*) *Pearl formation.* The belief that oyster pearls are caused by sand grains is only partly true; in fact, pearl formation is the standard reaction of many bivalve molluscs to the presence of an irritant. One of the commonest sources of such irritation is parasitic larvae, chiefly the cercariae and metacercariae of flukes. It is a little ironic that many of the most highly valued pearls are nothing more than 'ornamental parasites'!

Pearl formation is one of the better understood invertebrate reactions, investigated because of its commercial importance. Pearls are formed by concentric layers of nacre being deposited on the irritant, gradually producing a smooth, less irritating surface. Nacre is the name given to the calcium carbonate layer of pearls and characteristic in the mother-of-pearl of bivalve shells such as oysters.

(*ii*) *Parasitic castration and sex reversal,* Parasitic castration is another well-documented and dramatic result of infestation, best known from parasitic crustaceans. The common shore crab, *Carcinus maenas*, is not infrequently infected with the cirripedian parasite, *Sacculina* (Fig. 23).

A crab infected with *Sacculina* ceases to moult, owing to a hormonal upset, and can, therefore, be recognized by the flora and fauna on its carapace. Because it stops regular moulting, the weeds, barnacles and other epizooites begin to accumulate on the crab shell.

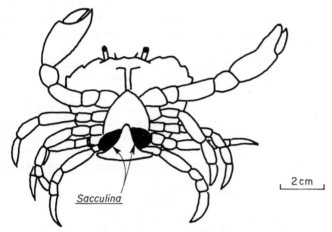

Fig. 23. *Sacculina* (Crustacea Cirripeda). It is parasitic on the shore crab *Carcinus maenas*. *Sacculina* sends 'roots' into the tissues interfering with metabolism and often causing 'parasitic castration'. One of the effects is to interfere with moulting and parasitized crabs can readily be recognised by the rich growth of epiphytes and epizoites on their carapace.

Sacculina does not appear to kill the crab, and certainly hosts have survived for over two years with the infection. In some cases however the parasite may grow into and destroy the gonads, and a sex reversal from male to female follows. Little is known of the physiological details of this reversal but the blood of a parasitized crab has a high lipid (fat) level. Normal females carry a higher level of fat than normal males, and parasitically feminized males have a fat level closer to that of the normal female.

The phenotypic, or structural appearance of the crab, frequently shows altered secondary sexual characteristics, always changing from male to female.

Another bizarre, although not infrequent, ectoparasite is the cirripede, *Peltogaster paguri*, found on the abdomen of the hermit crab, *Eupagurus bernhardus*. Sex reversal also occurs in the crab host of this parasite. Female crabs do not appear to be masculinized, and any sex reversal is always from male to female, as in *Sacculina*.

Intersexes of wasps have resulted from stylopoid hymenopterous parasites, and some authorities consider that the parasite may effect the sex determiner, which would normally dominate. The result of this is that the latent determiner of the opposite sex is able to exert its effect and cause a partial reversal of sex. In many insect hosts, those secondary sexual characteristics which are formed latest in development, are the first to be affected by the parasite. There is some evidence to suggest that

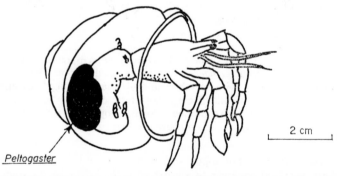

Peltogaster

2 cm

FIG. 24. *Peltogaster*. A crustacean parasite of the hermit crab *Eupagurus bernhardus*. It is a conspicuous (often over 1 cm.) yellow or pink parasite on the abdomen after removal from the adopted shell. A process facilitated by holding a flame under the apex of the shell.

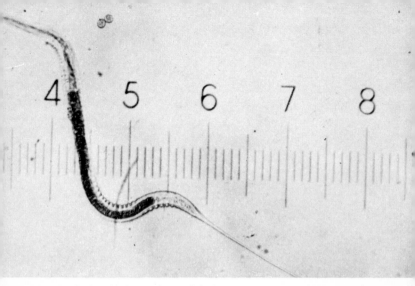

PLATE 3(a). Infective third stage larva of the horse nematode *Trichonema* (each division = 0.01 mm). Note the 'sheath' or retained second stage larval cuticle, thrown into folds. These can be readily recovered from week-old horse dung.

PLATE 3(b). A section through the anterior end of *Pomphorhynchus laevis* (Acanthocephala). The plate shows the proboscis embedded in the intestinal muscosa of the fish host, and the proliferation of cells in the host reaction.

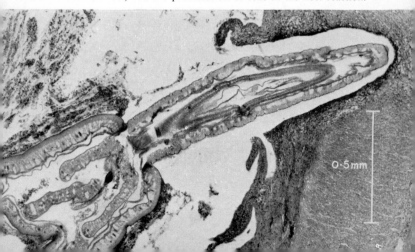

0·5mm

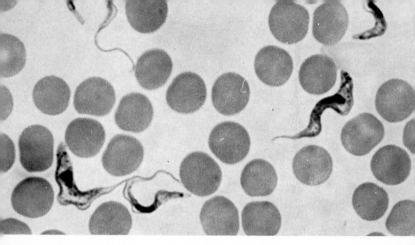

PLATE 4(a). A smear of rat blood infected with *Tyrpanosoma rhodesiense* (Protozoa), the causative organism of East African sleeping sickness in man. It is transmitted in nature by the tse-tse fly *Glossina morsitans*, and is confined to the south-eastern coastal areas of Africa.

PLATE 4(b). A smear of human blood showing a microfilaria of *Wuchereria bancrofti* (Nematoda), the causative organism of 'Elephantiasis'. The microfilariae show diurnal periodicity, being concentrated in the peripheral blood at night, a time that coincides with the feeding of the mosquito intermediate host *Culex fatigans*.

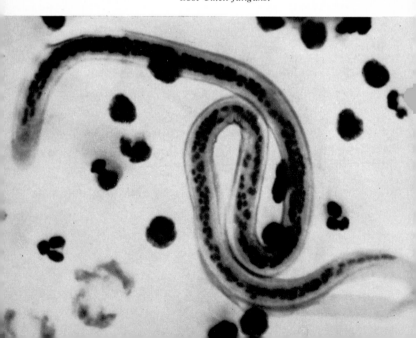

nutriment is the basic cause of sex reversal in insects, as it may be in crustaceans.

(*iii*) *Abnormalities of behaviour, colour and size.* In the discussion of transmission in Chapter 4 it was suggested that parasites exercise an influence on their hosts, which tends to isolate them and make them conspicuous. This they do by changing the host's behaviour, colour or size. *Leucochloridium* in snails, *Ligula intestinalis* (Fig. 19) in fish and *Cryptocotyle lingua* (Fig. 18) in snails and then in fish, have all been discussed.

To emphasize the fact that parasites can have an effect on their host's behaviour, one further illustration will be given.

A small and rather obscure group of parasites called the horse-hair or gordian worms (Nematomorpha) are parasitic in insects during their larval stages.

The eggs are laid by the free-living adults, which are not infrequent in ponds or horse troughs (from whence they were originally named), and a tiny armed motile larva escapes and penetrates into an insect. The insects used as hosts are usually grasshoppers, but can include beetles, bees, and wasps. When the larval parasite is about to mature, although still inside the insect, it must return to water and burst out of the insect, to live briefly as an adult, mate and lay its eggs.

It will be clear from the résumé of the life history that a major difficulty in the parasite's life is the return to water. It is, therefore, of particular interest that the parasite appears to affect the behaviour of its host, and 'encourages' it to return to water. The mechanism by which this is achieved is obscure, but there are sufficient isolated reports to certify that the parasite does influence its host, and often suicidally for the host.

One of the more dramatic reports describes an infected bee flying over a pool and, when about six feet over it, diving straight into the water. Immediately on impact the gordian worm burst out and swam into the water, the maimed bee being left to die.

Snails carrying fluke larvae are frequently found to be considerably larger than uninfected individuals (Rothschild, M.,

1941): it is not certain whether this is due to a preference on the part of the miracidium to infect a bigger snail, but it is probably due to the direct mechanical effect of the parasite burden exerting a pressure on the inside of the developing whorl. Another suggestion is based on the attraction of the miracidia to the mucus trail of the snail, the bigger snails producing more mucus and therefore picking up a greater infection.

Parasites can therefore cause abnormalities not only of behaviour and colour but also of size; it is important to realize that, by isolating the host, many of these abnormalities confer a definite ecological advantage on the parasite.

CYST AND GALL FORMATION

Cyst formation was shown above to be a vertebrate host reaction to infestation; similarly, galls and cysts are part of the invertebrate host reaction. *Myzostomum* (an aberrant annelid), parasitic on feather stars, is characteristically found in small cysts; and some of the less known molluscan parasites of tunicates (sea squirts) frequently evoke localized tissue responses of their hosts. Although outside the immediate scope of this book, it may be stressed that gall formation is not limited to animal hosts, and is also found in a number of plants. The familiar wayside oak galls caused by insects; the root knots of tomatoes produced in response to invasion by the plant-parasitic nematode, *Meloidogyne*; and the nodules formed on the roots of leguminous plants are all part of the host reaction in plants.

IMMUNITY

Edward Jenner in the eighteenth century was the first man to demonstrate conclusively the principle of immunity, using his vaccine against smallpox. In modern times, the principle he discovered is used extensively in human and veterinary medicine, but the mechanism of immunity is a complex biochemical subject, and its explanation is still largely hypothetical.

The immunity response is very much a chemical reaction; it

is a reaction between an antigen and an antibody. The antigen is the name given to the trespassing foreign body, a protein or a polysaccharide; the antibody is the product of the host response. The antibody is a compound known as a globulin with a molecular weight of about 160,000; it is a globular protein of blood plasma which can be identified as belonging to the faction known as 'gamma globulin'.

The orthodox immunity theory holds that the antibody is a compound produced in response to the antigen, which combines with it and, therefore, renders it harmless. Each antibody is capable of reacting only with the antigen which stimulates its production (R. S. Speirs, 1964).

The centre of host–antibody reaction is probably in the lymphocytes, which are one of the groups of white corpuscles. It is believed that these can make a protein template or pattern, which can be arranged in molecular correspondence to an antigen. The antigen, with its particular molecular configuration, is taken in by the lymphocyte and a 'molecular print' is taken. Against this print a counteracting and complementary print is made – the antibody (Fig. 25). Armed with knowledge of the original antibody structure the lymphocyte is able to produce large quantities of antibody, which is then released into the bloodstream and circulates with the serum. Every unit of antibody thus produced is able to combine with antigen identical with that originally taken up. The body then produces astronomical numbers of globulin protein antibody units which render harmless the foreign proteins by reacting with them and neutralizing their effects.

Such a highly specialized biochemical reaction is a very restricted one, with each antigen inactivated only by its own specific antibody.

The immunity response not only renders the antigens harmless but produces an excess of antibody which remains in the blood and confers an 'immunity', in some cases for life,* This form of protection being known as an 'acquired immunity'.

* This being the reason that people very rarely get measles, mumps or chickenpox more than once.

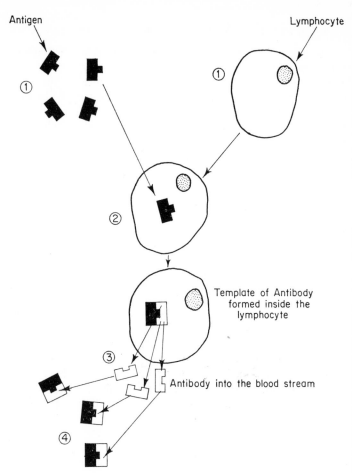

Antigen

Lymphocyte

① ①

②

Template of Antibody
formed inside the
lymphocyte

③

Antibody into the blood stream

④

Antibody neutralising the antigen in the blood serum

FIG. 25. A greatly simplified summary of the immunity response. An *antigen* (a foreign protein or polysaccharide) enters the blood stream and is taken up by a lymphocyte. The lymphocyte then produces a molecular template in correspondence to the antigen call an *antibody*. Having produced the template or mould, it can then release antibodies into the blood stream, which 'neutralize' the antigen in the serum.

Acquired immunity may be natural or artificial, depending on whether the above reaction occurs in the host itself, or not. In many cases immunity is acquired either by inoculation, or by vaccination, against a particular disease; the first of these gives an artificially acquired immunity, the latter a naturally acquired immunity.

If man is vaccinated, he is given a small or weakened dose of a disease, in response to which he forms an antibody and is thereafter protected from infection, but in some cases, this practice may be too dangerous, so the disease is given instead to a horse, cow, or other suitable animal. The lymphocytes of the horse then form an antibody, which may be extracted and centrifuged out of the horse's serum, and later injected into man's bloodstream, giving him an artificially acquired immunity by inoculation.

Immunity is a generalized host reaction and may be used equally against the particular proteins of parasites or against any foreign isolated proteins. Some allergies are believed to be caused by an activity of the immune reaction in response to a harmless chemical, for example hay fever may be caused by an immunity response to pollen grains, which once started gives a reaction every time the subject comes into close enough contact with pollen.

In the discussion on hyperinfestation and disease (Chapter 10) it is shown that parasitic immunity is a mutually beneficial response to the host–parasite relationship, for it permits a small level of infection but actively prevents a large infection or hyperinfestation.

This brief survey has listed some of the more important effects that hosts and parasites have on each other. It has also stressed that the long established and successful host–parasite relationship is one of mutual toleration, where neither partner exercises a major advantage over the other.

The very existence of a host–parasite relationship is a partial upsetting of the equilibrium of the individual host or parasite itself, that is, the association itself places a stress on both organisms. If the host–parasite relationship is to be considered as an equilibrium, the diverse reactions of host and parasite are little more than attempts to restore the original individual state. Taken to its natural conclusion, this attempt, if successful, leaves both host and parasite as near their normal individual selves as possible – this is the successful host–parasite' relationship.

9

The Worldwide Distribution of Parasites

Geographical limits

IT is a well-documented fact in studies of animal distribution that tropical regions of the world are populated by a great variety of creatures, whereas the temperate and polar regions, while often supporting large numbers, have relatively few different species. For an illustration of this, one has only to compare the desolation of the Arctic snows or Icelandic tundra with the teeming masses of life in the equatorial jungles of the Amazon or Central Africa.

This principle is also applicable to the zoogeography of parasites (Figs. 26 and 27). Part of the reason for this is intimately linked with the distribution of other animals which act as hosts. Parasites which depend on their hosts for an essential part of their existence are naturally limited to the regions of host occurrence. Regions where large numbers of hosts are found will also contain large numbers and varieties of parasites.

Parasites are restricted to the limits of their host range, and if they require more than one host in their life cycle, they are restricted to regions where both hosts occur. *Schistosoma*, the blood fluke of man, is prevalent in many parts of Africa, America, and the Orient, but cannot occur in Britain because the correct snail intermediate host is not present.

Two sets of ecological factors limit the worldwide distribution of parasites, for in addition to finding hosts for their parasitic stages, they must also be able to tolerate the conditions met with in their independent phases.

The juveniles of trichostrongylid nematodes rapidly succumb at temperatures below freezing point and direct exposure to ultra-violet radiation is fatal to almost all parasites (Rose,

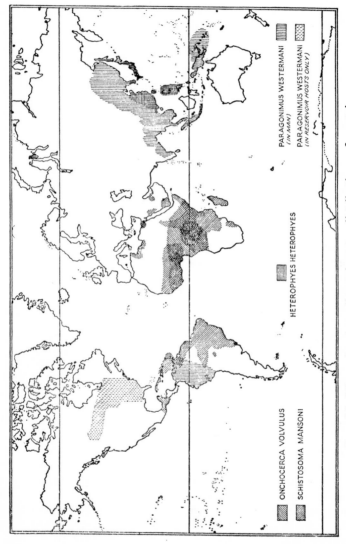

FIG. 26. Map showing discontinuous distribution of certain helminth parasites of man.

PARAGONIMUS WESTERMANI *(IN MAN)*

PARAGONIMUS WESTERMANI *(IN RESERVOIR HOSTS ONLY)*

HETEROPHYES HETEROPHYES

ONCHOCERCA VOLVULUS

SCHISTOSOMA MANSONI

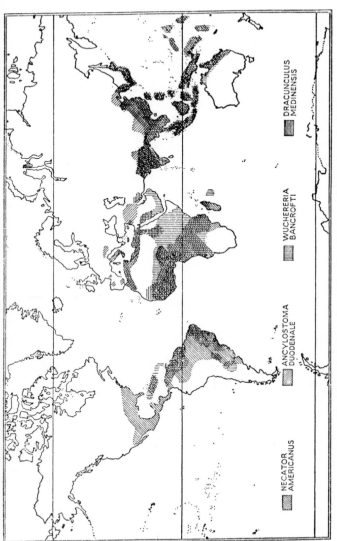

NECATOR
AMERICANUS

ANCYLOSTOMA
DUODENALE

WUCHERERIA
BANCROFTI

DRACUNCULUS
MEDINENSIS

FIG. 27. Map showing the wide distribution of certain helminth parasites of man.

1957). Temperature, light, humidity, and other physical and chemical factors must be adequate before development can proceed. If either of these phases, i.e. that inside the host or that outside the host, is unsuitable then the parasite will not survive.

Man's parasites are naturally affected by his location and the general conditions of the areas where he lives. When studied broadly the peoples of equatorial and subtropical regions are not only found in dense numbers, but include tribes and races which are often backward and lack the advantages of modern hygiene. In addition, tropical regions provide a wide range of the insects, molluscs, and crustaceans so important as intermediate hosts and vectors of protozoan and helminthic diseases.

A belt of human parasitic disease occurs around the equator and gradually lessens towards the poles. The reason for this is the combined effect of population habits and density, the suitability of external conditions for the independent stages of parasites, and the abundance of intermediate hosts and vectors.

Man's movements and activities

Throughout the course of history the geographical distribution of parasites has been affected by the mass movements of populations. In this way infection has been carried across oceans and mountains, spreading minute organisms over all the world.

To survive in a new habitat, parasites must be introduced in certain minimum critical numbers. During mass movements a sufficiently high nucleus of infection is present to persist in a new area. The slave trade, which exported thousands of natives from the African continent to the West Indies and Southern North America, provided such an opportunity for the spread of parasitic disease.

Among the parasites which the slaves carried were the blood protozoan *Trypanosoma vivax* and the hookworm *Necator americanus* (nematode). The former requires an insect intermediate host for transmission whereas the latter has a direct life cycle. Of the two only *Necator* persisted and spread throughout the Americas; *Trypanosoma vivax*, not having a suitable intermediate host never survived and is still found only in the limits of the tsetse fly belt of Central Africa.

The Great Lakes of North America provided an ideal habitat for *Diphyllobothrium*, the large tapeworm of man, but before the arrival of infected people it was not found there. Immigrants from the Baltic arrived in sufficiently high numbers to produce a level of infection able to persist. Imported Chinese labourers added to this and set up a thriving focus of infection which survives today. There are numerous other examples, often in times of war, when population movements have carried parasites throughout the world.

Man's local activities have also affected the incidence of parasites, as for example in Egypt. Bancroftian filariasis caused by *Wuchereria bancrofti* used to be prevalent throughout Egypt but is now restricted to a narrow belt of land bordering the Nile Delta. The intermediate host of this parasite is the mosquito *Culex fatigans*, which breeds in wells and in the still water of ponds. Irrigation channels and pipes decreased the number of available breeding places for the mosquito and consequently reduced the range and incidence of the disease.

The advent of irrigation however provided ideal conditions for the breeding of snails, these being the intermediate hosts of *Schistosoma haematobium*, which has consequently increased in Egypt. The sanitary habits of the Egyptians, together with the increase of intermediate hosts, has made schistosomiasis* the major medical problem of Egypt.

Hoare (1957), in a very interesting paper, described the spread of African trypanosomiasis beyond its natural range. *Trypanosoma brucei* is found in tropical Africa between 15° N. lat. and 25° S. lat., the limits of tsetse fly distribution. *T. evansi* which is morphologically similar to *T. brucei* has omitted the stages in the tsetse fly and has developed mechanical transmission by horseflies (family Tabanidae). Consequently it has been

* Schistosomiasis is the name of the disease caused by *Schistosoma*.

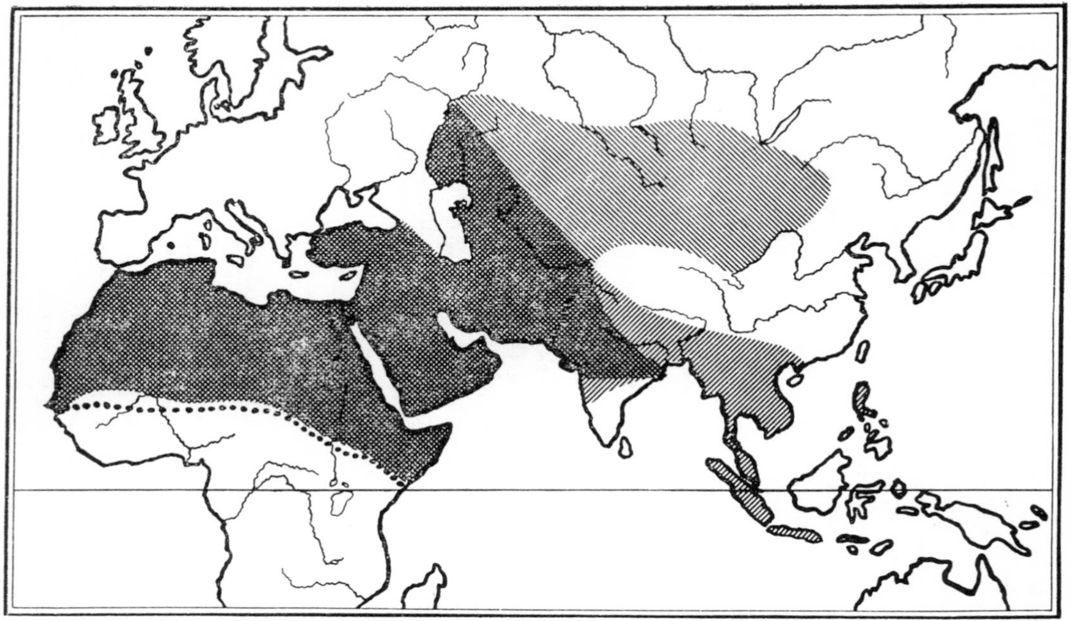

FIG. 28. Geographical distribution of Surra (*T. evansi*) and camels in the Old World.

▨ = range of Surra; ░ = range of camels; • • • • • • = northern boundary of tsetse-zone.

emancipated from the limits of the tsetse fly and spread into other continents (see Fig. 28).

T. evansi causes 'surra' in domesticated animals, especially horses, cattle, and camels; it occurs in Panama, South America, Asia to 53° N. in Russia, all of south China and in Africa as far as the Equator.

The southern boundary of *T. evansi* distribution is the northern limit of the tsetse fly belt. Camels travel across this boundary and carry *T. brucei* into the *T. evansi* regions, and it is believed that the camel has been instrumental in the spread of surra. The one-humped camel *Camelus dromedarius* has for centuries been the major beast of burden and means of communication throughout North Africa and Western Asia. The boundary of *T. evansi* and of this camel are remarkably similar. Thus man by his movements and communications has spread surra throughout the Old World. It was stated above that *T. evansi* was also found in Panama and Central America; man was again instrumental in its transport to the New World. Surra also parasitizes cattle and horses in addition to camels, and was carried across the Atlantic in the infected horses of the Spanish conquistadors in the sixteenth century. On returning, the same Spanish conquistadors are thought to have introduced the venereal diseases syphilis and yaws into Europe.

The parasites man shares with his domesticated animals

The continual contact between man and his associated animals has given ample ecological opportunity for the mutual exchange of parasites. It is from this source that man has become host to many of his most important pathogens.

Man's commonest parasite, *Ascaris lumbricoides*, infests 644 million persons out of an estimated world population of 2,167 million (Stoll, 1947). A morphologically similar, but distinct race of *A. lumbricoides* infests pigs and there is little doubt that continual contact with the pig provided the source of man's infection. *Necator americanus* of man also has a corresponding species *Necator suilla* in pigs. Pigs also share an amoebic parasite with man, *Iodamoeba butschlii*, and are involved in the transmission of trichinosis and the pork tapeworm *Taenia solium*. Human contact with the pig has been responsible for many parasites of man; it is not without reason that Mohammedans are not permitted contact with pigs!

Children frequently contract the parasites of their cat and dog pets, and man can become seriously ill with the disease of psittacosis from contact with birds of the parrot family.

Echinococcus granulosus, popularly known as the dog tapeworm, is found in the adult form in dogs and wild canines, its larval stages being spent in the sheep among other hosts. The larval stage is a cyst which may lodge in almost any organ of the body of the sheep, and buds off larval tapeworms internally, called the hydatid cyst (Fig. 29).

Man has become incorporated into the life cycle of this worm by providing an alternative host for the hydatid normally found in sheep, and strictly speaking has become an intermediate host of the dog tapeworm.

Hydatidosis, as the condition is called, is largely coincident with sheep farming. Australia, New Zealand, Tasmania, and parts of Africa and the Middle East are all areas of high incidence. The pathogenic effects of hydatidosis in man depend on the type and location of the cyst, but it may prove very serious and can only be effectively cured by surgery (see Fig. 29).

Echinococcus multilocularis has a very restricted range in Europe and North Asia, with a high level of infection among the Eskimos on St Lawrence Island in the Bering Sea. The principal definitive host is the wild fox or dog and the intermediate host in Europe is the field mouse, or another small rodent. Unlike many helminth eggs the eggs of *E. multilocularis* are very resistant to cold, remaining viable at temperatures as low as minus 56° C.

In areas bordering the Arctic Circle, dogs are used for hauling sledges and foxes are hunted commercially – the contact between man and the canine is frequent and intimate. If one

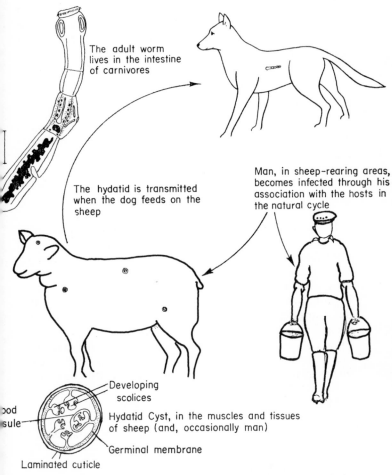

The adult worm lives in the intestine of carnivores

The hydatid is transmitted when the dog feeds on the sheep

Man, in sheep-rearing areas, becomes infected through his association with the hosts in the natural cycle

Developing scolices

Hydatid Cyst, in the muscles and tissues of sheep (and, occasionally man)

Germinal membrane

Laminated cuticle

ood sule

FIG. 29. *Echinococcus granulosus* (Cestoda). The natural cycle is between a carnivore and a ruminant. Man can enter the cycle through his contact with the infection, and often does so in sheep rearing areas.

may be teleological the ecological contact has been exploited by *E. multilocularis* and a successful cycle has been established between man and his dog. Although the infection goes no farther when in man, in this case it is his contact with dogs that causes the human disease Hydatidosis.

Conclusion

The varying physical and climatic conditions over all the world impose general limits on the geographical distribution of parasites. Most parasites require for the survival of their free-living stages, a critical level of humidity, a sufficiently high temperature for development, and a concentration of hosts adequate to ensure successful transmission. These factors are of prime importance in limiting the global spread of parasites.

The fundamental importance of temperature and humidity has largely restricted distribution to tropical and sub-tropical areas (see Figs. 26 and 27) for it is here also that the invertebrates necessary for the dissemination of disease are found in the greatest numbers. These regions furthermore are populated by primitive peoples, and it would therefore be expected that the distribution of human parasites would centre around the equator and decrease towards the poles, the exceptions being those parasites with direct life cycles, and resistant eggs which are not restricted by climatic factors or by the deficiency of intermediate hosts, e.g. *Ascaris* and *Trichuris* (the whip-worm of man).*

In his role as the dominant species on this planet, man has exerted a major influence not only over the zoogeography of his own parasites, but also over the range of the parasites of his domesticated animals.

* *Ascaris* and *Trichuris* are worldwide in distribution.

10

Hyperinfestation and Disease

THE upsetting of the host–parasite equilibrium in the immediate favour of the parasite, owing to its increase in numbers is termed hyperinfestation. The *immediate* nature of the advantage is stressed for the apparent advantage to the parasite is only temporary, an unhealthy host harbours unhealthy parasites. Hyperinfestation is not therefore considered to be a victory for the parasite, but rather a catastrophe. It is an upsetting of the host–parasite equilibrium, which leads to disease of the host. Disease in the present context is considered to be the direct result of parasitic hyperinfestation.

Throughout the course of the evolution of parasites it would be expected that the disadvantages of hyperinfestation would have been eliminated, and that the selecting forces of evolution would have favoured adaptations which tended to prevent hyperinfestation. If the causes and dangers of hyperinfestation are studied, parasitism can be regarded in a new light, considering the correlation between hyperinfestation and disease.

Parasitism has been described as 'invasion with compromise' (Noble). To be teleological: it is the aim of the parasite to tap the resources of its niche without inflicting major difficulties on its host. 'Parasites must not kill the goose that lays the golden eggs', or to quote a famous parasitologist: 'The parasite must live off interest and not capital.'

Parasitic fecundity

One of the basic characteristics of many parasites is that they lay enormous numbers of eggs. The chief reason has been explained as the need to overcome the hazards of the free-living existence, and successfully to reach another suitable host. The hazards and problems involved have been discussed in Chapters 2 and 3, and it is intended here to make a wider survey of the consequences and effects of the hazards and of the gross egg production.

There are two numerical factors to be considered which are in opposition. Just as an equilibrium exists between host and parasite, so there is an equilibrium between the number of parasite eggs and larvae produced, and the hazards of successful transmission. It is of fundamental importance to realize that the vast numbers of eggs produced are *essential* for the parasite's survival. This numerical adaptation has not been evolved to produce a superabundance of infective stages; it meets, in contrast, the bare requirements of survival. Just enough eggs are laid to overcome the natural toll of transmission, and successfully to propagate the next generation.

Before advancing the theme of this discussion, the two principles already mentioned must be firmly established. Firstly, it is harmful to a parasite to provoke a state of disease by parasitic hyperinfestation of its host. Secondly, the vast numbers of eggs produced by parasites (*Ascaris* for example laying 100,000 eggs per day) are only just sufficient to counterbalance the hazards they must meet.

There exist a number of phenomena in the biology of parasites, which can be interpreted as adaptations to avoid hyperinfestation of the host.

The inclusion of the independent stage in a life cycle disperses the parasite, while avoiding hyperinfestation. By preventing development and maturation of the parasite's young in the same host as the adult, the numbers parasitic in a single host are greatly restricted.

Immunity

Acquired immunity (see Fig. 25), in which a protective antibody is produced by the host in response to infective proteins (antigens) is the most widespread and probably the most effective method of avoiding hyperinfestation. In many cases of parasitism there exists a build-up of antibody in the host's blood, directly proportional to the build-up of parasites. When sufficiently high antibody level is reached, the host is immune and has a resistance to further parasitic infection. Such a mechanism ensures that a level of infestation is reached, after which no more parasites are able to enter the host successfully.

In practice this reaction is a method which permits a small infestation but prevents hyperinfestation. When viewed in this light acquired immunity is seen to be a delicate means of control, which is a parasite-evoked, host-limiting mechanism to prevent infection from reaching the level at which it causes disease.

Self cure

Another mechanism which prevents hyperinfestation is known as 'self cure'. Self cure is a phenomenon first observed by Stoll (1928), and elucidated by Soulsby in the nematode *Haemonchus contortus*.

Haemonchus contortus occurs as an adult in the stomach of sheep and the infective larval stage enters the host as a contaminant of grass while the host is grazing (see Fig. 30). On entering the stomach the infective larva burrows deep into the lining mucosa of its host's gut, and it is upon this habit that self cure depends. It stays in the mucosa for only a short time, before returning to the lumen and taking up blood feeding; but while in the mucosa it is in close proximity with the host's blood system. It is while the larva is near the blood system that there is a rise of the histamine concentration in the blood. The nearness of the larva to the host's blood also evokes an antibody response.

If a sheep infected with *Haemonchus contortus* adults is given a further or 'challenge' infection of infective larvae, the effect is to make the adults release their hold and pass out in the faeces.

The antibody and histamine circulates in the bloodstream and is taken in by the blood-feeding adults. Presumably the antibody or histamine has a sufficiently harmful effect to kill the adults.

Every time a previously infected host becomes reinfected with more larval stages of *Haemonchus contortus*, there is a replacement reaction, the challenge dose (as the second infection

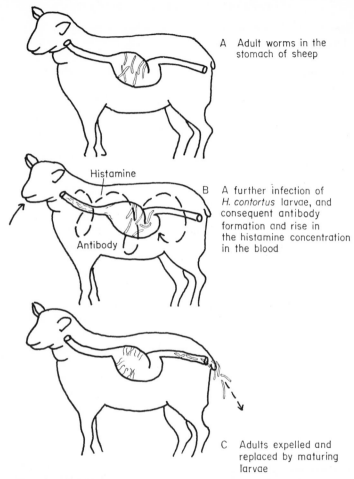

A Adult worms in the stomach of sheep

B A further infection of *H. contortus* larvae, and consequent antibody formation and rise in the histamine concentration in the blood

C Adults expelled and replaced by maturing larvae

FIG. 30. Self cure in *Haemonchus contortus* (Nematoda). Adult worms live in the stomach of sheep; when a further or 'challenge' dose of larval worms enters the gut they provoke an increase in histamine in the blood and stimulate formation of antibody. This forces the adults to release their hold and pass out, to be replaced by the maturing larvae (a kind of parasitological musical chairs!).

is called) forcing out the old adults and taking their place. The effect of the self cure reaction is to prevent a level of hyperinfestation from building up in the host which would otherwise result from a continued increase of *Haemonchus contortus* numbers. Similar reactions have been demonstrated in the rodent nematode *Nippostrongylus brasiliensis*.

Direct competition

Ackert, in 1931, illustrated another ecological principle in the avoidance of hyperinfestation. Experimenting more recently with the nematode *Ascaridia lineata*, he showed that by feeding chicks with varying numbers of nematode eggs and larvae, the percentage of hatching and rates of growth varied inversely with the number of eggs fed. To summarize, the smaller number of eggs gave a higher percentage of hatchings and a greater growth rate in the worms. If many eggs were fed to the chicks, only a small percentage of them hatched and the worms which developed were small. The reason for this was probably the competition between the worms themselves. Competition among parasites is yet another ecological factor which limits parasitic hyperinfestation.

In the case of those parasites that come into contact with the bloodstream, it is apparent that hyperinfestation is likely to be prevented by the formation of antibody. Lumen dwellers of lungs, gut, bladder, etc., that do not come into contact with the bloodstream are unlikely to provoke an immune reaction. It would seem that in lumen parasites the chance of hyperinfestation would be greater. It is therefore of particular interest that there should exist features in the biology of some lumen parasites which seem to guard against hyperinfestation.

Staggering the Sites of Parasitization

In the gut of sheep are found a large number of closely related nematode parasites, and each is found inhabiting a particular region shared only with a few others.

Another impressive example of the staggering of the points

of parasitism is found in the protozoan *Eimeria*, some species of which cause coccidiosis in poultry (Fig. 31). There are eight distinct species of this genus found in different regions of the fowl's gut and, although the ranges of some overlap, each is characteristically found infecting only a limited area.

If a parasite is forced out of its usual habitat into a slightly different area and survives, it never attains the same size or egg output as in its optimum niche.

The phenomenon of sharing out the area for parasitization avoids hyperinfestation of any single tissue or organ system; this results in the maximum number of parasites exploiting the greatest area of the host, with the minimum amount of harm being inflicted on any one organ.

Parasite-mix

Another ecological feature which has scarcely been investigated is the inter-relationships between the parasites of a single host. The term 'Parasiticoenosis', introduced by Pavlovski, is defined

TABLE 2. The positions occupied by the nematode parasites of the alimentary canal of the sheep

Nematode	Organ
Haemonchus contortus	Abomasum
Ostertagia circumcincta	Abomasum
Trichostrongylus axei	Abomasum
Trichostrongylus colubriformis	Duodenum
Strongyloides papillosus	Duodenum
Nematodirus filicolis	Small intestine
Bunostomum trigonocephalum	Small intestine
Cooperia curticei	Small intestine
Oesophagostomum colubriana	Colon
Trichuris ovis	Caecum

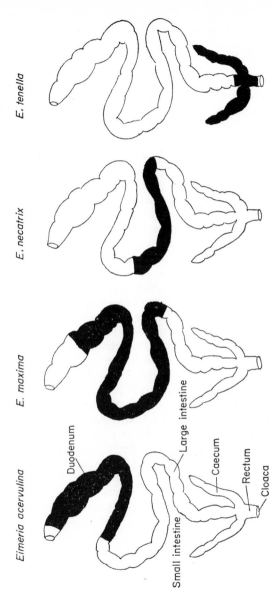

FIG. 31. Staggering the sites of parasitization. Not infrequently it is found that closely related parasites occupy different regions of an organ system. One of the best examples is that of the protozoan coccidian genus *Eimeria*, some of which are parasitic in the gut of the fowl.

as 'All animals and bacteria, inhabiting all the *biotopes* within the same host.' Noble (1960) has suggested the alternative phrase 'Parasite-mix', which has a similar meaning.

As the host provides the microenvironment of the parasite, it is clear that there will be competition and antagonism between the various members of the host's parasitic fauna. Ackert (p. 109) showed the effect of competition between eggs and larvae in a single species, *Ascaridia lineata*, but antagonisms also occur between unrelated parasites.

In addition to the direct aspects of competition, e.g. the search for a vacant area of attachment, or the unfavourable effects of concentrated excretory products, or even direct competition for food, there appears to be a complex range of antagonisms between distantly related parasites.

Wilson, as long ago as 1916, saw that an antagonistic relationship existed between parasitic copepods and the glochidia larvae of fresh-water bivalve molluscs. He found that fish infected with copepods rarely or never had glochidia larvae, and similarly if glochidia larvae were to be found, there were no parasitic copepods. Both the glochidia larvae and the copepods are found all over the fins and gills as ectoparasites of fish, and it is unlikely that the antagonism is due to direct competition for a site. The mechanism of control of such a phenomenon is not clear, but the phenomenon itself is well established.

Scheuring (1923) pointed out that acanthocephalans are usually absent from the gut of fish infected with the tapeworm *Triaenophorus nodulosus*. Both these examples, and the example following, are antagonisms between separate phyla. Other examples have also been recorded between copepods and monogenetic trematodes.

Noble *et al.* (1963), in an intensive survey of the parasites of the mudsucker *Gillichthys mirabilis*, has attempted to apply statistical methods to his extensive data. Unfortunately, he could show no certain antagonisms between the parasites but he did show that the sex of the host could be an important factor in controlling parasitic infection. Of the four parasites (2 flukes, a copepod and a protozoan) investigated, a larger number of female fish had 3 species and a disproportionately large number of male fish were infected with 2 or fewer species of parasite.

This largely unexplored field of ecology, the interrelation between parasites in a parasite-mix, may show in time that parasites have direct biochemical or physiological effects on one another. Already there is enough evidence to show that, in some cases, the incidence of one parasite affects the incidence of another.

This whole idea of inter-relations between members of a parasite-mix, however, may be interpreted as a way of avoiding disease of the host by hyperinfestation. It is a means of preventing heavy parasitic burdens of distantly related animals, which could not otherwise be controlled by acquired immunity or direct competition for site or food.

Other more general aspects of the biology of parasitism may be interpreted as methods of avoiding hyperinfestation. Very rarely do parasites enter their hosts by more than one route. The three main routes being: contaminatively (on the food); by direct penetration of the skin; or by inoculation by ecto-parasitic vectors. These routes very rarely overlap, and each parasite is adapted to one only.

Host specificity

Host specificity (see Chapter 6) is one of the most interesting and fundamental phenomena of parasitism. Its origin has already been traced along two lines of specialization, those of phylogeny and ecology. The occurrence of host specificity is undisputed and its origin is largely agreed upon, but few authors attempt any explanation. The mechanism by which host specificity arose is not the issue here; we are not concerned with *how* it came about but rather *why* it came about.

Taking a wider view again, so as to see host specificity in perspective, it is postulated that the phenomenon of host specificity was able to develop because it was selected, or rather the advantage it carried was selected during the course of evolution.

Closely related hosts harbour closely related parasites (see Fig. 21) and hyperinfestation is avoided by the acquired immunity of the host. But hyperinfestation is again a danger when parasites sufficiently distantly related not to evoke similar antibody production, are competing for sites on the same host. This difficulty is overcome by the demands of specialized physiology and morphology which are the tolerance limits of host specificity.

Host specificity, therefore, creates yet another superimposed barrier, which avoids hyperinfestation by closely related parasites not otherwise limited by the same antibody. Host specificity may have come about as a mechanism preventing extensive parasitic hyperinfestation.

One of the more far-reaching problems of parasitism, and possibly the most important of all to a successful and well-adapted parasite, is that of host disease resulting from parasitic hyperinfestation. It has been shown in this section that a number of the characteristics of parasitism may have evolved to avoid this problem.

Man's influence

When considered in the most general terms, hyperinfestation is seen to be disadvantageous to both host and parasite; furthermore, the selecting forces of evolution would have protected parasitism from its dangers. Any biological features which tends to avoid hyperinfestation, would be favoured by selection and consequently developed and incorporated in the biology of parasites.

The parasitic existence is beset with hazards, but there is an element of conservatism about parasites, which protects them against a possible and suicidal degree of success. Evolution (to be highly teleological) has equipped parasites with the capacity for taking advantage of the host but the good sense not to be greedy.

Parasitic infestation is often correlated with disease when really hyperinfestation is the offender. Parasites are adapted to avoid hyperinfestation and it is often man's own doing when a disease level of parasitic hyperinfestation is reached.

If man, by his modern methods of husbandry, agriculture, and civilization, removes the natural limiting factors which have been paramount in moulding the biology of parasites and in the past have developed parasites which produce vast numbers of eggs, he will be upsetting the equilibrium of the ages. By concentrating his crops, his cattle, and himself, he is reducing the hazards of the parasite, and preventing the environment from taking its natural toll. In the place of natural equilibrium, man is substituting ideal conditions for the spread and multiplication of parasites and, consequently, of disease by parasitic hyperinfestation. The close proximity of the hosts, their restricted pastures and the removal of the difficulties of transmission and infection has been neatly summed up in a famous piece of alliteration 'permanent pastures perpetuate parasites'.

Man has caused the upsetting of the natural equilibrium by an unnatural concentration of himself, his farm animals, and his farm crops; he has imposed an artificial set of factors which has aided the dispersal and transmission of parasites. The advent of man's civilization has carried with it a biological disturbance which has caused disease by hyperinfestation. It is not the parasites but man who has been a chief factor instrumental in causing the diseases found today.

It is not without cause that the quotation 'a disease of civilization' has come into our everyday jargon.

Parasitism is an ecological relationship which is precariously balanced between extinction by natural hazards, and extinction by complete success, and in the natural state there exist adaptations which enable both extremes to be avoided.

Most of what has been said in the preceding pages has been rather general, and was intended to present a somewhat theoretical background to the way of life of parasites. It is hoped that the interested student may himself attempt to collect and identify environmental parasites or those encountered during routine laboratory examinations. Because of the difficulties that may be met with in the identification and preparation of slides, a short appendix follows which may be of some assistance.

For more detailed identification the books listed in the bibliography should be consulted.

Appendix 1

Laboratory Techniques

The fixing, preserving, and mounting of helminths

ACANTHOCEPHALA, CESTODA, AND TREMATODA

1. Fix in warm (not boiling) AFA.* If the material is alive it is liable to contract and become contorted; to prevent this, fill the test tube almost to the top with AFA, warm and put in the worm; shaking violently for about one minute. This shaking causes sufficient turbulence to relax the worm by making its muscular contractions useless. Leave in AFA for at least 24 hours, and for larger worms for up to a week.

2. Then store in a mixture of 70% alcohol with 5% glycerine – for as long as required.

To stain.

1. Stain overnight in alcohol carmine hydrochloride, or borax carmine, or a nuclear haematoxylin stain.

2. Differentiate in acid alcohol for several hours.†

* Chemical	Quantity
40% Formalin	100 ml.
95% Alcohol	250 ml.
Glycerine	100 ml.
Glacial Acetic Acid	50 ml.
Distilled water	500 ml.
	1000 ml.

† To differentiate equally the whole length of a tapeworm is often a problem, as the thin end with the scolex clears more rapidly than the thick end; to overcome this difficulty use the method shown in Fig. 32.

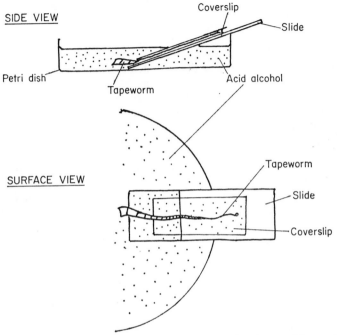

FIG. 32. When staining tapeworms, there is the problem of equal differentiation over all the body. This may be done as shown above, where the scolex is held in a thin film of acid alcohol, while the heavier segments are suspended freely in excess acid alcohol.

3. Blue in alkaline 70% alcohol or take through 50%/30% alcohol to distilled water and take up to 70% again, thus 'blueing' in tapwater.

4. Take up to 90% and absolute alcohol for complete dehydration (for 2–4 mins).

5. Clear in methyl benzoate, or xylene (for 2–3 mins).

6. Mount in balsam.

NEMATODA

Kill and fix in warm 70% alcohol or 5% formalin and store in 70% alcohol. To stain nematodes is a great problem, and it is usually adequate to clear them in lactophenol. For permanent preparations the worm should finally be placed in dehydrated glycerine and the coverslip sealed with nail varnish.

If a stain is required, suitable temporary staining is achieved by placing a *very small* drop of cotton blue in the lactophenol, and observe in this mixture of cotton blue–lactophenol. Permanent preparation should not be made with lactophenol, as the slides may go black after a period of time.

After clearing and observing in lactophenol, if the nematode is wanted, it should be returned to 70% alcohol. Large nematodes can often be more effectively cleared in beechwood creosote.

Appendix 2

Key to the General Identification of Helminths

Key

(1) Oval or elliptical	(3)
(2) Elongate	(5)
(3) Posterior sucker with hooks or clamps, almost always parasitic on the skin or gills of fish	Monogenoidean Fluke
(4) Anterior sucker around the mouth, and ventral sucker of variable position; usually mid-ventral. Neither type of sucker ever has clamps or hooks. Always endoparasitic, commonly in the gut of all classes of vertebrates.	Digenean Fluke
(5) With spiny, retractible proboscis, unsegmented.	Acanthocephala (spiny headed worm)
(6) With very small scolex with hooks or suckers at the narrow end of the tapering body; segmented.	Cestoda (tapeworm)
(7) Without obvious suckers or spines, often curled up, usually pointed at one end (the tail). Either the posterior end cf the male, or the anterior end of either sex may be developed into a *small* cone. May be found in many organs of any vertebrate and almost any invertebrate.	Nematoda

FAECAL ANALYSIS

The usual and most accurate method of investigation is that of direct dissection and observation; but it is possible that the

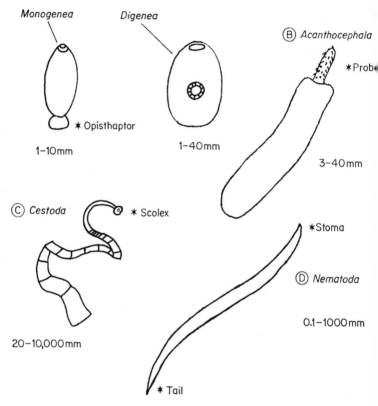

(A) *Trematoda*

Monogenea

Digenea

* Opisthaptor

1–10 mm

1–40 mm

(B) *Acanthocephala*

* Probo

3–40 mm

(C) *Cestoda*   * Scolex

20–10,000 mm

* Stoma

(D) *Nematoda*

0.1–1000 mm

* Tail

* Denotes key structures of importance
  in further identification

FIG. 33. The detailed identification of helminths is often a
specialist's job, depending on a knowledge of the important
features (among others) those denoted in this diagram. The figure
shows the four major groups of helminths, and with the key
provided, should make it possible broadly to group any that
may be found.

host animal concerned is not dead and may not be killed or is to be released, as for example in a mammal trapping survey.

The importance of dung and droppings as the starting point of a parasite's free-living existence, has previously been emphasized; dung contains the most concentrated mass of eggs and larvae to be found outside the host.

If mature egg-laying parasites are present, their eggs may be in very large numbers and the distinction between the eggs of the main groups of helminths is not difficult, but to identify the egg down to generic level (as can often be done with experience) is not as easy.

A word of warning about confusing eggs with other similarly sized objects should be included. Fungal spores, protozoan cysts, undigested food particles such as the setae of earthworms, and even air bubbles may readily be mistaken for helminth eggs by the hasty (or even sometimes by the skilled) observer.

To investigate the dung, the usual method is a faecal smear:

1. Place the dung in a mortar, add water, and work with the pestle to a thick cream. To concentrate, mix the dung in a test tube and add 51% saturated zinc sulphate solution, shake and centrifuge, fill up to top and then place a coverslip over the top of the test tube. The eggs will float up onto it. Leave for 30 minutes and remove coverslip, placing it on a slide for examination.

2. Examine a smear in water.

Permanent preparations. 3. Smear a coverslip with glycerine or horse serum; then add a thin smear of dung and place face down for 20 minutes in Schaudinn's fluid.*

4. 70% alcohol to wash.

5. 70% alcohol and iodine solution to remove the mercuric chloride.

6. 70% alcohol with a few drops of 1% sodium thiosulphate to remove the yellow colour of iodine.

* Schaudinn's fluid – Mercuric chloride (saturated aqueous soln.) 2 parts (20 ccs.) Absolute alcohol, 1 part (10 ccs.). Glacial acetic acid, 1 drop.

If a stain is required, Ehrlich's haematoxylin is a satisfactory nuclear stain. Then dehydrate, clear in xylene, and mount in balsam as before.

This method is used largely for protozoan oocysts, and the alternative for helminth eggs is to clear them in glycerine and mount in glycerine jelly.

Ectoparasitic insects

During the examination of small mammals, birds, and even bats, a number of ectoparasitic arthropods will be found. Mites and ticks are readily recognized, as having four pairs of legs, the other ectoparasites, with three pairs of legs, are all insects.

Fleas are common on almost all warm-blooded vertebrates, some having a high degree of host specificity, while others retain a wide host range. Another group of ectoparasitic insects which is commonly found on birds is the Mallophaga, or biting lice, which are also found, although less frequently, on mammals. The last and possibly rarest group of insects that may be collected belong to the family Nycteribiidae and are found exclusively on bats. These are closely related to the sheep 'ked', and a number of other related ectoparasites occur on horses, wild birds, and deer.

In all these cases, it is a good idea to put the dead host on to a piece of white paper, so that the small ectoparasites will easily be seen. If permanent preparations are to be made the following method may be used:

1. Place the insect in cold 10% NaOH or KOH solution, which clears away the tissues, leaving only the cuticle.

2. Wash in clean or distilled water.

3. If placed directly in alcohol, the insect will become brittle and unmanageable, so it is important to place it carefully on a slide in a position which shows all its structure to advantage. Place in a very small drop of water, on a slide, and cover with a coverslip. After having positioned the insect, run a number of

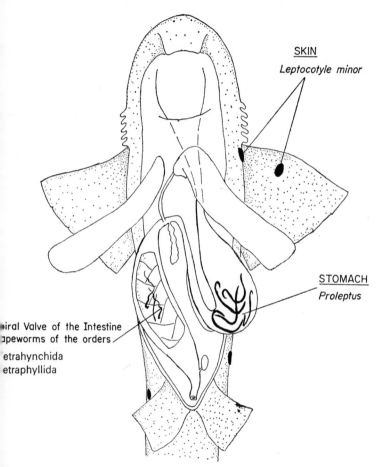

SKIN
Leptocotyle minor

STOMACH
Proleptus

▸iral Valve of the Intestine
⸱apeworms of the orders
⸱etrahynchida
⸱etraphyllida

FIG. 34. A map of the common helminths of Dogfish. *Leptocotyle minor,* may well be mistaken for a piece of mucus, while in a close examination of the spiral valve small cotton-like cestodes may be found. In the writer's experience almost all Dogfish are infected with the nematode *Proleptus,* a parasite they harbour through eating the infective stage present in crabs.

changes of 90% alcohol over it. This will cause it to become fixed in the desired position.

4. Dehydrate in absolute alcohol.

5. Clear overnight, or until completely clear in clove oil.

6. Wash quickly in xylol.

7. Mount in balsam.

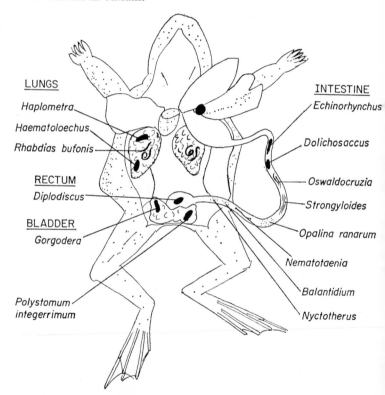

Fig. 35. A map of the common parasites of the frog. The frog is always infected with *Opalina ranarum* and frequently has helminths in the lung.

Appendix 3

Summary of the Parasites Mentioned in the Text

I⊤ has been necessary in the previous chapters to make references to a wide spectrum of parasitic forms. In order that the reader, who is unfamiliar with them, should not get lost, a brief list of the parasites, with their hosts, location and Zoological Class, is given.

Genus	Definitive Host	Location	Intermediate Host(s)	Zoological Class
Ancistrocephalus	Polypterus (a lung fish)	Intestine	? probably a copepod	Cestoda
Ancylostoma	Mammals (man)	Small intestine		Nematoda
Anopheles	Warm blooded verts	Skin		Insecta
Ascaridia	Warm blooded verts (chicken)	Small intestine		Nematoda
Ascaris	Warm blooded verts (man)	Small intestine		Nematoda
Azygia	Carnivorous fish (perch)	Intestine	Snail, Small fish	Trematoda (Digenea)
Babesia	Cattle	Blood	Tick	Protozoa
Balantidium	Vertebrate	Large intestine		Protozoa
Boophilus	Cattle	Blood		Acarina
Bunostomum	Herbivora (sheep)	Small intestine		Nematoda
Capillaria	Mammals and birds	Small intestine		Nematoda
Centrorhynchus	Carnivorous birds	Small intestine	Insects, small mammals	Acanthocephala
Cleripes	Horseshoe bats	Skin		Pupipara insecta
Cooperia	Mammals (sheep)	Small intestine		Nematoda
Crassicauda	Cetacea and rats	Urino-genital tract		Nematoda
Cryptocotyle	Shore birds (gulls)	Bursa fabricae	Snail and herring	Trematoda (Digenea)
Cysticercus	See Taenia			Cestoda
Cystoopsis	Fish (sturgeon)	Subcutaneous tissue	Parasitic Oligochaete	Nematoda
Diclidophora	Marine fish (hake)	Gills		Trematoda (Monogenea)
Dictyocaulus	Ruminants (cow)	Lungs		Nematoda
Dientamoeba	Man	Intestine		Protozoa
Diplodiscus	Amphibians (frog)	Rectum	Snail	Trematoda (Digenea)

Genus	Definitive Host	Location	Intermediate Host(s)	Zoological Class
Diplozoon	Freshwater fish (minnow)	Gills		Trematoda (Monogenea)
Discocotyle	Marine and freshwater fish	Gills		Trematoda (Monogenea)
Dolicosaccus	Frog	Intestine	Snail	Trematoda (Digenea)
Dracunculus	Verts (man)	Connective tissue	Copepod	Nematoda
Echinococcus	Canines (dog)	Small intestine	Ruminants (hydatid)	Cestoda
Echinorhynchus	Frogs	Small intestine	Insects	Acanthocephala
Eimeria	Large range of verts	Intestine		Protozoa
Enterobius	Man	Rectum		Nematoda
Fasciola	Herbivora (sheep)	Liver, bile duct	Snail	Trematoda (Digenea)
Fecampia	*Idotea neglecta*	Abdomen		Turbellaria
Glochidia larvae	Freshwater fish	Skin and fins		Mollusca
Glossina	Warm blooded verts	Skin		Insecta
Gordian worms	Insects	Abdomen		Nematomorphida
Gorgodera	Common frog	Urinary bladder	Snail	Trematoda (Digenea)
Haematoloechus	Common frog	Lungs	Snail	Trematoda (Digenea)
Haemonchus	Sheep	Stomach		Nematoda
Haplobothrium	Bowfin	Intestine	? probably Copepod	Cestoda
Haplometra	Common frog	Lungs	Snail	Trematoda (Digenea)
Helobdella	Fish (sole)	Skin		Hirudinea
Herpetomonas	Insects (house fly)	Small intestine		Protozoa
Heterakis	Birds	Small intestine		Nematoda
Heterodera	Solanaceae (potatoes)	Roots		Nematoda
Histomonas	Domestic fowl	Intestine, caeca, liver	(*Heterakis*)	Protozoa
Hydatid	See *Echinococcus*			
Hystrichopsylla	Warm blooded host	Skin		Flea, Insecta
Ichneumon	Insect, larvae	Body cavity		Insecta
Iodamoeba	Mammals (man)	Intestine		Protozoa
Kuhnia	Marine fish (mackerel)	Gills		Trematoda (Monogenea)
Lankesterella	Cold blooded verts (frogs)	Endothelial blood cells	Blood-sucking inverts	Protozoa
Leptocotyle	Selachian (dogfish)	Skin		Trematoda (Monogenea)
Lernaeocera	Cod	Gills	Flatfish	Crustacea
Leucochloridium	Birds (jay)	Rectum	Snail	Trematoda (Digenea)
Ligula	Piscivorous verts	Intestine	Copepod, fish	Cestoda
Loa loa	Mammals (man)	Connective tissues	Blood-sucking fly	Nematoda
Mallophaga	Warm blooded verts	Skin and feathers		Insecta
Meloidogyne	Solanaceae (tomato)	Roots		Nematoda
Myzostomum	Crinoidea	Axils of arms		Annelida
Necator	Man, Chimpanzee, pig	Small intestine		Nematoda
Nematodirus	Mammals (sheep)	Intestine		Nematoda

Genus	Definitive Host	Location	Intermediate Host(s)	Zoological Class
Nematotaenia	Amphibia (frog)	Large intestine		Cestoda
Nippostrongylus	Rodents (rats)	Small intestine		Nematoda
Nyctotherus	Amphibia (frog)	Colon		Protozoa
Oesophagostomum	Mammals (sheep)	Intestine		Nematoda
Ollulanus	Cats	Stomach		Nematoda
Opalina	Amphibia (frogs)	Rectum		Protozoa
Ornithorhynchus	Birds	Skin		Insecta
Oswaldocruzia	Frogs	Small intestine		Nematoda
Ostertagia	Mammals (sheep)	Stomach		Nematoda
Paragonimus	Man (Asia)	Lungs	Snail	Trematoda (Digenea)
Peltogaster	Hermit crab	Skin of abdomen		Crustacea
Phytomonas	Plants	Latex	Hemipterous insect	Protozoa
Plectanocotyle	Fish	Gills		Trematoda (Monogenea)
Plasmodium	Mammals, birds and reptiles	Erythrocytes	Insects, mosquitoes	Protozoa
Polystomum	Frogs	Urinary bladder		Trematoda (Monogenea)
Proleptus	Selachians and tortoises	Stomach		Nematoda
Rhabdias	Amphibia (frogs)	Lungs		Nematoda
Sacculina	Shore crab	Throughout body	Plaice	Crustacea
Schistosoma	Mammals (man)	Hepatic portal vein, and bladder	Snail	Trematoda (Digenea)
Strongyloides	Verts (man)	Intestine		Nematoda
Spirocerca	Carnivores	Tumour, lungs		Nematoda
Syngamus	Birds and mammals	Trachea		Nematoda
Syphilis	Man	Cerebro-spinal fluid		Spirochaeta
Taenia	Carnivorous mammals	Intestine	(Cysticercus) herb. or omniv. mam.	Cestoda
Toxocara	Carnivorous mammals	Intestine		Nematoda
Triaenophorus	Carniv. fish (pike)	Intestine	Copepod, fish	Cestoda
Triatoma	Warm blooded mammals	Skin		Insecta
Trichinella	Most mammals (rats)	Intestine		Nematoda
Trichomonas	Verts and inverts	Various organs		Protozoa
Trichonympha	Termites and woodroaches	Intestine		Protozoa
Trichostrongylus	Mammals, rarely birds	Intestine		Nematoda
Trichuris	Mammals (man)	Intestine		Nematoda
Trypanosoma	Various verts (man)	Blood	Glossina	Protozoa
Wuchereria	Lymph nodes and blood	Mosquito		Nematoda

Bibliography

(Those references marked thus * are textbooks recommended for further reading.)

1. Ackert. (1931.) 'Quantitative studies on the administration of variable numbers of nematode eggs (*Ascaridia lineata*) to chickens' *Trans. Amer. micro. Soc.* **50**. (3), 206–214.
2. Baer, J. G. (1952.) *Ecology of Animal Parasites.* University Illinois Press.
*3. Cameron, T. W. M. (1956.) *Parasites and Parasitism.* Methuen, London.
4. Cameron, T. W. M. (1964.) 'Host specificity and the evolution of helminth parasites.' *Advances in Parasitology 2.* Edit. B. Dawes. Academic Press, New York and London.
5. Cleveland, L. R. *et al.* (1934.) 'The Wood-feeding roach, *Cryptocercus*, its Protozoa, etc.' *Mem. Amer. Acad. Arts. Sci.* **17**. 185–322.
*6. Dawes, Ben. (1956.) *The Trematoda.* Cambridge University Press.
7. Dunning, W. F. and Curtis, M. R. (1946.) Multiple peritoneal sarcoma in rats from intraperitoneal injections of washed ground *Taenia* larvae. *Cancer Research* 13. 838–842.
*8. Dogiel,V. A. (1961). *Parasitology of Fishes.* English trans. Z. Kabata. Oliver and Boyd, Edinburgh.
9. Gibbs, B. J. (1962.) 'The Occurrence of the Protozoan Parasite *Histomonas meleagridis* in the Adults and Eggs of the Cecal worm *Heterakis gallinae. J. Protozoology.* **9**. 288–293.

10. Hawking, Frank. (1965.) 'Advances in filariasis, especially concerning periodicity of microfilariae.' *Trans. R. Soc. trop. Med. Hyg.* **59**. 1. 9–21.

11. Heitz, A. (1918.) '*Salmo salar*, seine Parasitenfauna und seine Ernährung im Meer und im Süsswasser.' *Arch. Hydrobiol. XLL.* 2–3.

12. Hoare, C. A. (1957.) 'The spread of African Trypanosomes beyond their natural range.' 2. *Tropenmedizin und Parasit.* **8** ($\frac{1}{2}$). 5 pp.

13. Knorre, A. G. (1937.) 'The distribution of parasites in their hosts, and the problem of specificity.' *Ann. Leningr. Univ. XIII.* Ser. biol III. 4.

*14. Kudo, R. R. (1960.) *Protozoology* (4th edition). Charles C. Thomas, Illinois.

15. Llewellyn, J. (1958.) 'The adhesive mechanisms of monogenetic trematodes: the attachment of species of the Diclidophoridae to the gills of Gadoid fishes.' *J. Mar. Biol. Ass. U.K.* **37**. 67–79.

*16. Noble, E. R. and G. A. (1961.) *Parasitology: The Biology of Animal Parasites.* Lea and Febiger, Philadelphia.

17. Noble, E. R. (1960.) 'Fishes and their parasite-mix as objects for ecological studies.' *Ecology.* **41**. No. 3. 593–6.

18. Noble, E. R. *et al.* (1963.) 'Ecology of the gill parasites of *Gillichthys mirabilis.* Cooper. *Ecology* **44**. No. 2. 295–305.

19. Pavlovski, E. N. (1937.) 'The concept of biocoenosis in application to some parasitological problems.' (In Russian) *Bull. Acad. Sci., U.S.S.R.*

20. Robinson, J., Poynter, D. and R. J. Terry. (1962.) 'The role of the fungus *Pilobilus* in the spread of the infective larvae of *Dictyocaulus vivipans.*' *Parasitology* **52**. 17–18.

21. Rogers, W. P. (1960) (The physiology of infective processes of nematode parasites; the stimulus from the animal host) *Proc. Roy. Soc.* B 152: 367–386.

*22. Rogers, W. P. (1962.) *The Nature of Parasitism.* Academic Press, New York.

23. Rose. (1957.) 'Observations on the bionomics of the free-

living first stage larvae of the sheep lungworm *Muellerius capillaris.' Journal of Helminthology* **31**. 1–2.

24. Rothschild, M. (1941.) *Parasitology* **33**. 406–415.
25. Rothschild, M. and Clay, T. (1952.) *Fleas, Flukes and Cuckoos.* Collins, London.
26. Scheuring, L. (1923.) 'Studien an Fischparasiten. I. *Triaenophorus nodulosus* (Pall.). Rud. und die durchihn im Fischkörper hervorgerufenen Veränderungen. *Zeitschr. Fisch. XII.*
*27. Smyth, J. D. (1962.) *Introduction to Animal Parasitology.* E.U.P., London.
28. Speirs, R. S. (1964.) 'How cells attack antigens.' *Scient. American,* Feb.
29. Stoll, N. (1947.) 'This Wormy World.' *J. Parasitology* **33**. 1–18.
30. Taylor, A. E. R. (1965.) 'Evolution of Parasites.' *Third Symposium of the British Society for Parasitology.* Blackwell, Oxford.
*31. Von Brand, T. (1952.) *Chemical Physiology of Endoparasitic Animals.* Academic Press, New York.
32. Wesenberg-Lund, C. (1931.) 'Contribution to the development of Trematoda Digenea.' Part I. The biology of *Leucochloridium paradoxum. D. Kgl. Dansk. Vidensk. Selsk. Skfifter. Naturw. Math. Afd. Raekke.* **4**. (3). 90–142.
33. Wallace, H. R. (1961.) 'The bionomics of the free-living stages of zoo-parasitic and phyto-parasitic nematodes, a critical survey.' *Helminthological Abstracts* **30**. 1–22.
*34. Wallace, H. R. (1965.) *The Biology of Plant Parasitic Nematodes.* Arnold, London.
*35. Watson, J. M. (1960.) *Medical Helminthology.* Baillière, Tindall and Cox, London.
36. Yorke, W. and Maplestone, P. A. (1926.) *The Nematode Parasites of Vertebrates.* Churchill, London.
37. Wardle, R. S. and McLoed, J. A. (1952.) *The Zoology of Tapeworms.* University of Minnesota Press.

Index